S0-AWK-295

# Dust of Her Feet

## Reflections on Amma's Teachings

### VOLUME 2

By

Swami Paramatmananda Puri

Mata Amritanandamayi Center
San Ramon, CA

**DUST OF HER FEET**
Reflections on Amma's Teachings
Volume 2

By Swami Paramatmananda

Copyright © 2015 by Mata Amritanandamayi Center
All rights reserved.

No portion of this book, except for brief review, may be reproduced, stored in a retrieval system, or transmitted in any form or by any means—electronic, mechanical, photocopying, recording, or otherwise, without permission of the publisher.

Published by
Mata Amritanandamayi Center
P.O. Box 613
San Ramon, CA 94583-0613
USA

April 2015

# CONTENTS

DEDICATION.................................................................. 6

PREFACE........................................................................ 7

CHAPTER 1 — The True Guru ...................................... 9

CHAPTER 2 — Love vs Knowledge ................................ 17

CHAPTER 3 — Detachment ........................................... 23

CHAPTER 4 — Oneness with God.................................. 31

CHAPTER 5 — Childlike Innocence Towards the Guru........ 39

CHAPTER 6 — Kindness vs Selfishness ............................ 49

CHAPTER 7 — Peace is Our True Nature .......................... 57

CHAPTER 8 — The Unique Purpose of Human Birth.......... 65

CHAPTER 9 — The Need for Renunciation....................... 81

CHAPTER 10 — Vasanas ................................................ 89

CHAPTER 11 — Witnessing ............................................ 103

CHAPTER 12 — Yearn for God........................................ 111

CHAPTER 13 — Be Childlike, Not Childish ...................... 115

CHAPTER 14 — Work Should Become Worship................. 121

CHAPTER 15 — The Great Power of Maya ....................... 135

CHAPTER 16 — God is the Doer...................................... 147

CHAPTER 17 — Wake Up, Wake Up! ............................... 157

CHAPTER 18 — Surrender and Detachment ...................... 167

CHAPTER 19 — Truthfulness and Responsibility .............. 183

CHAPTER 20 — Man—the Glory of Creation.................... 191

# DEDICATION

*Salutations to*
*Sri Mata Amritanandamayi Devi,*
*the Universal Mother,*
*the Dispeller of misery from the world,*
*the One who chases away the darkness*
*of Her devotees and displays Herself as the*
*Eternal Consciousness inhering in the Heart,*
*Who shines as the Transcendental Truth*
*underlying the world and beyond.*

# PREFACE

Since 1968, Swami Paramatmananda Puri has lived the life of a renunciate in India, having moved there at the age of nineteen, to imbibe the spiritual essence of that great and ancient culture. It has been his good fortune to have kept the company of many saints and sages over the years, culminating in his meeting with his Guru, Mata Amritanandamayi, in 1979.

When Swami first met Amma, he asked her how he should continue his sadhana. Amma's reply: "Become like the dust under everyone's feet." This is how this book's title came about.

As one of her senior disciples, he was eventually asked to return to the U.S. to serve as head of the first ashram in the West, the Mata Amritanandamayi Center in California, where he remained in residence from 1990 until 2001.

Many residents and visitors to the Center still remember that one of the high points there was Swami's talks, which encompassed his experiences in India, his understanding of Amma's teachings, scriptural texts, and his life on the spiritual path. With wit and humor, he has synthesized East and West and created a forum for spiritual learning for people from all walks of life.

Although Swami has not given any public talks since his return to India in 2001, many recordings of his satsangs have not yet been published. This book is an effort to share some of that material as well as some of his written articles after returning to India.

Publisher
M. A. Center
May 2015

# CHAPTER ONE

# The True Guru

When I came to Amma, I was very happy and peaceful, or so I had thought. But after settling down in the ashram, many negative thoughts and feelings began surfacing, such as doubt, anger and jealousy. It seemed to me that Amma was manipulating situations to bring out the worst in me, and, in fact, in everyone. On the one hand, it was blissful to be in Amma's Divine Presence, but it was extremely painful to be agitated much of the time. There were many times when I wanted to leave the ashram and go back to the peaceful village that I had been living in before coming to Amma. But I recognized that Amma was a divine being and probably the only person alive that could show me the way to the goal I desired. Her power of attraction was undeniable. But I had asked for peace, not suffering!

In my calmer moments, I gradually realized that what was deep inside me was simply coming out. I might have previously cleaned the surface of my mind, but Amma wanted to reach into the darkest corners and shake out the ghosts that were hiding there. There is a golden rule of spiritual life: what is inside must come out before we can enjoy real peace and bliss. The poison that has been swallowed in the past must be vomited out in order for us to become healthy. Amma cannot fill us with bliss when there are other dirty things in the vessel of our mind. How could I completely empty my mind? Certainly, not on my own. Somehow, circumstances must bring our innermost negativities to the surface of our mind so that they can be seen and dealt with at the conscious level. That is one of the Guru's jobs, to bring out what is within. A stiff brush is needed to clean a very dirty bottle. Amma says,

> "The Guru will create obstacles and sorrow for the disciple. The disciple should overcome all that with intense sadhana. Spirituality is not for idle people. The difficulties at the subtle level are hard compared to the sorrows of the external world. There is nothing to fear for one who dedicates everything to a Satguru."

Through association with a real Guru, we learn what should be discarded and what should be cultivated both within the mind and in our actions. The Guru's example becomes our guideline, our inspiration. But we should not stop there. We have to realize that every situation in our life is being manipulated by the Guru for our spiritual evolution. Nature is the servant of our Guru, who uses it for our spiritual development. Everything that happens to us is a chance to improve spiritually, for that is the real goal of human birth, Self-realization. If one develops this attitude, one is half way to the Goal. But it is not easy because we are so preoccupied with external affairs like eating, sex, socializing, making money and so on. We are like fish that cannot see the ocean because of being preoccupied with eating and not being eaten.

### Story of the Hidden Teacher

After many years studying spiritual subjects, a devotee felt that the time had come to travel in search of a direct experience of Reality. 'I will go,' he said to himself, 'seeking the Hidden Teacher, who is also said to be within my innermost self.'

Walking out of his house, he came upon a sadhu plodding along the dusty road and fell into step alongside him, waiting for him to speak.

Finally, the sadhu spoke. "Who are you and where are you going?"

"I am a seeker, and I am in search of the Hidden Teacher."

"I will walk with you," said the sadhu.

"Can you help me to find the Teacher?'

"The Hidden Teacher, so they say, is in a man's self. How he finds him depends upon what use he makes of his experiences. This is something I can only partly convey."

Eventually, they came to a tree, which was creaking and swaying. The sadhu stopped. "The tree is saying, 'Something is hurting me; stop awhile and take it out of my side so that I may find repose.'"

"I am in too much of a hurry," replied the other man, "and how can a tree talk, anyway?" So they went on their way.

After a few miles, the sadhu said, "When we were near the tree, I thought that I smelled honey. Perhaps it was a wild bees' hive that had been built in its trunk."

"If that is true, let us hurry back so that we may collect the honey, which we could eat and sell some for the journey."

"As you wish," said the sadhu.

When they arrived back at the tree, however, they saw some other travelers collecting an enormous quantity of honey.

"What luck we have had!" these men said. "This is enough honey to feed a city. We poor pilgrims can now become merchants; our future is assured."

Hearing this, the sadhu and his new found friend went on their way.

They then came to a mountain on whose slopes they heard a humming. The sadhu put his ear to the ground. Then he said, "Below us there are millions of ants building a colony. This humming is a concerted plea for help. In ant language it says, 'Help us, help us. We are excavating, but we have come across strange rocks that bar our progress. Help dig them away.' Should we stop and help, or do you want to hasten ahead?"

"Ants and rocks are not our business, brother," said the devotee, "because I, for one, am seeking my Teacher."

"Very well, brother," said the sadhu. "Yet they do say that all things are connected, and this may have a certain connection with us."

The young man took no notice of the older man's mumbling, and so they continued on their way.

The pair stopped for the night, and the youth found that he had lost his knife. "I must have dropped it near the anthill," he said. So, the next morning, they retraced their steps.

When they arrived back at the anthill, they could find no sign of the knife. Instead, they saw a group of people covered in mud, resting beside a pile of gold coins.

"These coins are a hidden hoard that we have just dug up. We were on the road, when a frail old holy man called to us and said, 'Dig at this spot and you will find that which is rocks to some but gold to others.'"

The young man cursed his luck. "If we had only stopped, you and I would have both been rich last night, O sadhu." The other party said: "This sadhu with you, stranger, looks strangely like the one whom we saw last night."

"All sadhus look very much alike," said the sadhu.

The two men continued their travels. Some days later, they came to a beautiful river bank. The sadhu stopped. As they sat waiting for the ferry, a fish rose several times to the surface and mouthed at them.

"This fish," said the sadhu, "is sending us a message. It says, 'I have swallowed a stone. Catch me and give me a certain herb to eat. Then I will be able to bring it up, and will thus find relief. O travelers, have mercy on me!'"

At that moment, the ferry boat appeared and the young man, impatient to get ahead, pushed the sadhu into it. The boatman was grateful for the pennies they were able to give him, and the two of them slept well that night on the opposite bank, where a generous soul had built a teahouse for travelers.

In the morning, they sat sipping their tea when the ferryman appeared. "Last night had been my most fortunate one," he said. "The pilgrims had brought me luck." He kissed the hands of the venerable sadhu, to take his blessing. "You deserve it all, my son," said the sadhu.

The ferryman was now rich and this was how it had happened. He was about to go home at his usual time, but he had seen the pair on the opposite bank and re-solved to make one more trip in order to get the blessing of helping poor travelers. When he was about to put away his boat, he saw the fish that had thrown itself on the bank. It was apparently trying to swallow a piece of a plant. The fisherman put the plant into its mouth, upon doing which the fish vomited a stone and flopped back into the water. The stone was a huge and flawless diamond of incalculable value and brilliance.

"You are a devil!" shouted the infuriated youth to the sadhu. "You knew about all these three treasures by means of some hidden power, yet you did not tell me at the time. Is that true companionship? Formerly, my ill-luck was strong enough, but without you, I would not even have known of the possibilities hidden in trees, anthills and fish, of all things!"

No sooner had he said these words thaen he felt as though a mighty wind was sweeping through his very soul. And then he knew that the very reverse of what he had said was the truth.

The sadhu touched him lightly on the shoulder and smiled. "Now, brother, you will find that you can learn by experience. I am he who is at the command of the Hidden Teacher."

And from that day onwards, the seeker was known by the name 'He who has Understood.'

# CHAPTER TWO

## *Love vs Knowledge*

We live in a technological age. Life used to be very simple and still is in some places. People lived simply, without electricity. Their bodies got sufficient exercise just by doing their daily chores. They were close to Nature. They knew the rhythms of Nature. They believed in the existence of God and had faith in Him. Their pleasures were simple and innocent and their minds had noble characteristics like humility, patience and self-sacrifice.

Then came electricity and technology. Now look at the present trend. People have so much pride. Where there is pride, there is anger and impatience. They are restless for something new all the time. T.V., the Internet, and various amusements occupy all their leisure time. The amount of selfish heartlessness and cruelty seem to be increasing all the time and no one is able to stem the tide of violence. From childhood onwards, one is bombarded with the false ideals of violence, anger, power, position and indiscriminant sex.

Technology, in itself, is not evil. But it should be used not just for the sake of efficiency, comfort and pleasure, but rather for instilling higher ideals. Just observe how one feels after seeing an uplifting movie. The effect may last many hours or even days. An inspiring book, which has come into our hands as the result of the development of the printing press, might change our life.

But, in general, technology has dried up the good qualities in most of us and made us overly intellectual. We depend on our intellect for everything. We have to know the why and how of everything. Faith has become weak or even non-existent unless, our intellect is satisfied. In a material sense, we have gained, but spiritually we are great losers. Happiness, to be lasting and satisfying, has to be in the heart, not in the head. It is the difference between knowing all the ingredients in a tasty dish and eating it.

As Amma says,

> "In today's world, people give more importance to the intellect than to the heart. This change is not very encouraging. Only if we cultivate an innocent and expansive heart, can we attain the Realm of God. This is not to say that the intellect has no place in our self-unfoldment. We need the head as well as the heart. Each has its own role to play in our growth. It is with the help of the intellect that we discriminate between what is wrong and what is right, between the real and the unreal, between the eternal and the ephemeral. But it has its drawbacks

also. It is like a pair of scissors. The nature of a pair of scissors is to dissect and discard. The intellect has not the broadness or expansiveness to encircle and accommodate everything. If we just go by the intellect, we will miss the sweetness of life. The heart, on the other hand, is like a needle. Its nature is to stitch and join things together. It accepts and unites even the most disparate and dissimilar things. It inspires us to see the good side of everything and imbibe the good in everything. Both the intellect and the heart are necessary to lead a harmonious life and to reach our eternal goal which is God. After we cut a piece of cloth into pieces of proper size and shape with scissors, we use a needle to stitch them together to create a shirt or blouse or dress.

"Our first prayer should be to develop a heart that rejoices in the happiness of others and shares their sorrow. God's real children are those who see the happiness and sorrow of others as their own."

With such an intellectual mind, we come to spiritual life, we come to Amma. We see in Amma what a blossomed heart truly means, and we feel our dryness in comparison. Still, our intellect, from past habit, becomes critical and judgmental, and it tries to measure and understand Amma instead of just basking in her presence. We might even miss the point of being with her.

### Knowing Versus Loving God

There was a pundit, in the olden, days who was well versed in all the scriptures. These scriptures did not at all satisfy the cravings of his mind, for he wanted to know nothing less than the whole of God. Finding no help in the scriptures, he went away to a solitary place far from the haunts of men, where he built a hermitage to devote himself entirely to realize the full knowledge of God. The hermit, whose desires were very few, devoted his whole day and night for the realization of the one desire of his heart. Days and months passed, but he could not understand anything about God.

Years rolled by, but the persevering and assiduous hermit remained as ignorant as before. Youth passed away and grey hairs began to appear amongst his long brown locks, and still, the problem remained unsolved just as before.

One day, he was walking on the beach with a dejected and pensive look, thinking about his unsuccessful struggle and considering whether he might give up the attempt or not, when, casting his eyes before him, he saw a little boy at some distance just on the brink of the water, busy with something. Thinking that a certain fisherman's child had been left there by its father, who had gone perhaps to the open sea to catch fish, but not satisfied as to why the father should bring such a little child from home and leave it there alone, he went to the child to inquire. The child, however, was quite unconscious of his approach, for it was very busy throwing water from the sea on the sands with its tiny hands. At such a novel sight, the curiosity of the sage was roused to its utmost degree, and he began to interrogate the boy as to who he was, why he was throwing water in that way, where his father had gone, and other things, to all of which the boy had no time to answer—the little creature was so engrossed in its apparently fruitless work. At last, the child, not wanting to be disturbed any longer, answered the sage once and for all, "Sir, I have no time to talk with you. Don't you see that I have to throw away all the water of this ocean and thus dry it up?"

"Are you mad?" asked the sage. "You, little creature, want to dry up the whole of this limitless ocean, which the whole human race together could never think of attempting?"

"Why, Sir," answered the child, "is it impossible for me to dry up this infinite ocean and see what is concealed in its depths, if it is possible for you to know and unravel the infinite profundity of God?"

With this, the child vanished from the spot and was seen no more. But his sweet words, which had found entrance into the pundit's heart, always rang in his ears and filled him with unspeakable joy. From that day onwards, he gave up his vain pursuit, and instead of trying to know God, he began to love Him.

# CHAPTER THREE

# *Detachment*

Those who have read Amma's books would have noticed that Amma puts a great deal of importance on detachment. We may feel as if Amma is telling everyone that they should become *brahmacharis* (celibates) or *sannyasis* (monks). In fact, it is not so. But she does want us to try to remain peaceful whatever the circumstances our fate throws at us. For most of us, any little disturbance at home or at work is enough to set us either worrying or going into a rage. We may feel that this is quite normal, since everyone is doing the same. But, in fact, Amma says that there is no need to become restless or miserable when circumstances change, or things don't go the way we wish they would, or people don't act according the way we would like. She says that we should not depend so much on outer things and people for our happiness. There is a unique spring of happiness within the mind of every living being, but it is not manifest; it is like butter in milk. One must work to get that treasure. But, if one succeeds, then nothing, not even sickness or death, can take it away. That permanent inner calmness is the real fruit of spirituality.

A foolish king complained that the rough ground hurt his feet, so he ordered the whole country to be carpeted with cowhide. The court jester laughed when the king told him of his order. "What an absolutely crazy idea, your Majesty," he cried. "Why all the needless expense? Just cut out two small pads of cowhide to protect your feet!" The Enlightened know that to make the world a painless place, you must change your heart, not the world.

There was a prince named Sri Rama in ancient India. The story of his life is called the *Ramayana*, and it has eternal value for any human being striving for lasting happiness and peace. He was the favorite of the subjects and of his father, the king. The king decided to make him the prince regent, the inheritor of the throne. When Rama was told the news, he smiled gently. The night before the installation ceremony, the king's other wife, Rama's stepmother, insisted that the king make her own son the successor to the throne and also to exile Rama into the forest for fourteen years! With great trepidation, Rama was informed of the decision the next morning, the day of his coronation. Gently smiling, he happily retired to the forest saying that he was very lucky that he would be able to spend so much time out in Nature and with the sages in their ashrams in the forest. He was not overjoyed at what was pleasant nor was he miserable about the unpleasant. He was even minded.

Look at Amma's life. She has faced so many obstacles and difficulties. She has never run away from even the most trying circumstances or responsibilities. She is truly every man's Guru. She knows what suffering is first hand. Currently, Amma does not have the same kinds of problems. She is very well known and respected in India. But now she has numerous responsibilities. There are orphanages, hospitals, schools, computer institutes, colleges, ashrams and temples. There are also hundreds of thousands of devotees all over the world expecting her guidance and protection. Yet, in spite of all this, Amma radiates peace at all times. That peace is unchanging and permanent, whatever may be happening around her.

How is Amma able to do all this without getting agitated? Because she does not look upon anything as her own. She considers everything as God's. This does not imply indifference but rather, detachment. Amma does everything as perfectly as possible, as a trustee of the Divine, but she directly perceives that all is His Will. We can only be instruments.

### Evenness of Emotions Due to Detachment

There was once a beggar in the ancient Indian city of Ayodhya. He lived by the side of the road in a hut made of gunny sacks and made his living by going from shop to shop begging from the merchants for a few pennies. He carried with him an old, rusty vegetable oil can, which he had found in a rubbish heap. Some of the merchants felt sorry for the man and used to regularly give him some coins whenever he passed by. They used to refer to him as the beggar with the oil can. To those, he extended his blessing and felt happy on receiving enough to buy some food. But others did not want to be bothered with him and used to abuse him and chase him away. He would feel dejected on those occasions and shower curses on those who turned him away. Thus, he was leading a miserable life of ups and downs.

One day, as he was going on his rounds, a car drove up, and four uniformed men got out. They walked over to the beggar, who, stricken with fear, bolted off. Hotly pursuing him, they finally caught hold of him, much to his chagrin. He pleaded with them to let him go, for he had neither harmed anyone nor had he stolen anything. Yet they would not heed his words and pushed him into the car. He neither knew who they were nor what they wanted with him. He felt that at least he was lucky in not receiving a beating, and so he kept quiet.

Soon, they pulled up to a palace and got out. Taking him into a room there, they took away his rusty can and tattered rags and, after bathing him in scented water, dressed him in royal finery. They then ushered him into the banquet hall and entertained him with a delicious feast, the likes of which he had never had in his entire life. As he came out of the hall, he remembered his oil can and tried to go to the bathroom where it had been left, but the servants obstructed his way. Annoyed, he said, "See here, why have you taken away my only possession? I do appreciate the fine meal you have given me and the nice clothes, but I want to go now. Therefore, please return my rags and the oil can this moment so that I may leave." The servants said, "My good man, a surprise awaits you. Your lucky days have begun. If you just contain yourself for a little while, you will understand why we are treating you like this." They then led him into the royal court where everyone there stood up and bowed to him.

The beggar was surprised. He thought that he was dreaming. He addressed them saying, "Sirs, I don't know why you are bowing down to me, but you are driving me crazy with this kind of treatment." The Prime Minister said, "Your Majesty, you are the heir to the throne. Kindly honor us by sitting on the throne now." The beggar said, "You are mistaken. I am only a beggar. These people have forcibly brought me here. I am not your king; therefore, please let me go back to my own place."

The ministers said, "Your Highness, you do not know your own lineage. You are the rightful heir to the throne. When our king died childless, we tried to trace his heir in the royal family. After a thorough investigation, we found that a distant relative of the king, while going through a forest with his wife and only child, was waylaid by some robbers and deprived of his life along with his wife's. Only the child was spared and left to its fate. The child had a mole on its left ear and a scar on its right foot. A couple days later, the king came to know of the murder and had a thorough search made for the child, but to no avail. When the king died recently, we also made extensive efforts to find the heir, and all clues led to you. It is really our good fortune that has brought the only surviving member of the royal line back to us. Therefore, please deign to accept our offer and rule over this country with righteousness."

Years passed, and the king happily ruled the kingdom. One day, as he was walking through the palace, he noticed a locked cupboard that he had never noted before. He asked for the key to be brought, and then opened it. What did he behold but his old oil can and tattered rags. A funny idea took hold of him. He locked the cupboard and kept the key. The next day, he took out the can and old clothes and put them into a suitcase. He then had the driver of his car bring the car and dismissed him for the day. Getting into the car with the suitcase, the king drove to the city where he used to beg. Stopping at the outskirts, he got out and changed his clothes. Walking through the streets with the can in his hand, the king-turned-beggar went on his old rounds. A few people recognized him as the beggar of many years back and gave him a few pennies. Others showered abuses on him and chased him away. Yet he neither felt elated with the former nor dejected with the later. He knew that he was, in truth, the king of the land. After a day of begging, he returned to the palace and resumed his duties as the king.

This is the state of one who has reached Perfection. He has conquered his mind and leads an equipoised existence. He knows himself to be the Infinite Bliss and is unaffected by the pleasures or pains of empirical life. His apparent joys and sorrows are only superficial waves passing over the eternal calm of his real Self. He has used every circumstance to make himself firmer and firmer in that unshakable state. That is the goal that Amma holds out to us. She shines as a perfect example of what she teaches.

# CHAPTER FOUR

# Oneness With God

Tens of thousands of people of all ages and from all walks of life come to see Amma from all around the world. And even though each one comes with a different desire, wish, need or fear, she ultimately holds out the same goal before all—the attainment of lasting happiness. Her presence and contact with her gives us a glimpse, a faint glimmer of that bliss.

Amma will satisfy most of our desires if she feels that they are good for us in the long run, but ultimately, she wants us to rise above satisfying desires as well as to let go of our fears, to reach the blissful state of samadhi. In fact, she knows that every one of us, whoever we are, can reach that sublime plane of existence. She does not discourage anyone in their pursuit of worldly goals, but says that, ultimately, only samadhi will satisfy the thirst of the soul. We may feel that attaining such a state is an impossibility for most of us. We are satisfied with our human condition. A little pleasure and not too many worries is enough for us. But Amma says that we are one with God, the Ocean of Bliss, even though we don't feel it now. Her mission in life is to awaken us to that truth, however long it may take. She sees Divinity in us, just as a sculptor sees a beautiful image in a piece of stone.

In her song, *Ananda Veethi*, Amma clearly tells us about her mission that was given to her by the Divine Mother:

> One day long ago, my soul was dancing in delight through the path of bliss. At that time, all of the inner foes such as attraction and aversion ran away and hid themselves in the innermost recesses of my mind.

> Forgetting myself, I merged in a golden dream that arose from within me. Noble aspirations clearly manifested themselves in my mind.

> The Divine Mother of the Universe caressed my head with bright, gentle hands. I stood respectfully with my head bowed and I told the Divine Mother that my life is dedicated to Her.

> Today, I tremble with bliss recollecting what Mother said. O Pure Consciousness, the embodiment of Truth, I will heed Your words!

> Smiling, She became a divine effulgence and merged in me. The events of millions of years gone by rose up within me.

> Mother told me to ask the people to fulfil the purpose of their human birth. My mind blossomed, bathed in the many hued light of divinity.

From that day onwards, I was unable to perceive anything as different or separate from my own inner Self, everything was a single Unity. Merging with the Divine Mother, I renounced all sense of enjoyment.

"O man, merge in your Self!" This sublime truth, which Mother said, I proclaim to the whole world. May this give refuge and solace to those who are overburdened with countless sorrows.

Thousands and thousands of Yogis have taken birth in the land of Bharat (India) and have lived these principles visualized by the great Sages of the ancient past. To remove the sorrows of humanity there are profound truths. "My darling child, leaving all other works; come to Me, you are always Mine."

Although Amma's advice may seem to be way beyond us, we should proceed along the pilgrimage of life, with faith in her, back to the blissful state of oneness with the Divine Being. More than anything else, faith is the power that will make it possible.

### The Caterpillar and the Butterfly

"Let me hire you as a nurse for my poor children," said a butterfly to a quiet caterpillar, who was strolling along a cabbage-leaf. "See these little eggs," continued the butterfly. "I do not know how long it will be before they come to life, and I feel very sick. If I should die, who will take care of my baby butterflies when I am gone? Will you, kind, mild, green caterpillar? They cannot, of course, live on your rough food. You must give them morning dew and honey from the flowers, and you must let them fly about only a little at first. Dear me! It is a pity that you cannot fly yourself. Dear, dear! I cannot think what made me come and lay my eggs on a cabbage-leaf! What a place for young butterflies to be born upon! Here, take this gold-dust from my wings as a reward. Oh, how dizzy I am! Caterpillar! you will remember about the food…"

And, with these words, the butterfly's wings became limp and she died. The green caterpillar, who had not had the opportunity of even saying "yes'" or "no" to the request, was left standing alone by the side of the butter-fly's eggs. "A pretty nurse she has chosen, indeed, poor lady!" exclaimed the caterpillar, "and a pretty business I have in hand. Why did she ever ask a poor crawling creature like me to bring up her dainty little ones! I am sure they'll mind me when they feel the wings on their backs and can fly away!"

However, the poor butterfly was dead, and there lay the eggs on the cabbage-leaf, and the green caterpillar had a kind heart, so she resolved to do her best. "But two heads are better than one," said she. "I will consult some wise animal on the matter." Then she thought and thought until at last she thought of the lark, and she fancied that because he went up so high, and nobody knew where he went to, he must be very clever and know a great deal.

Now, in the neighboring cornfield, there lived a lark. The caterpillar sent a message to him, begging him to come and talk to her. When he came, she told him all her difficulties, and asked him how she was to feed and rear the little butterfly creatures.

"Perhaps you will be able to inquire and learn something about it the next time you go up high," said the caterpillar timidly.

"Perhaps I can," answered the lark, and then he went singing upwards into the bright, blue sky, till the green caterpillar could not hear a sound, nor could she see him anymore. So she began to walk round the butterfly's eggs, nibbling a bit of the cabbage-leaf now and then as she moved along.

At last, the lark's voice began to be heard again. The caterpillar almost jumped for joy. It was not long before she saw her friend descend to the cabbage bed. "News, news, friend caterpillar!" sang the lark, "but you probably won't believe me! First of all, I will tell you what those little creatures should eat. What do you think it is? Just guess!" "Dew and honey out of the flowers, I am afraid!'" sighed the caterpillar. "No such thing, my friend," cried the lark. "You are to feed them with cabbage leaves!" "Never!'" said the caterpillar indignantly. "It was their mother's last request that I should feed them on dew and honey."

"Their mother knew nothing about the matter," answered the lark. "But why do you ask me and then disbelieve what I say? You have neither faith nor trust. What do you think those little eggs will turn out to be?"

"Butterflies, to be sure," said the caterpillar.

"Caterpillars!" sang the lark, "and you'll find it out in time." And the lark flew away.

"I thought the lark was wise and kind," said the caterpillar to herself, once more beginning to walk around the eggs, "but I find that he is foolish and saucy instead. Perhaps he went up too high this time."

Descending once more, the lark said, "I'll tell you something else. You will one day be a butterfly yourself!"

"Wretched bird," exclaimed the caterpillar. "You are making fun of me. You are now cruel as well as foolish! Go away! I will ask your advice no more."

"I told you that you would not believe me," cried the lark.

"I believe everything that it is reasonable to believe, but to tell me that butterflies' eggs are caterpillars, and that caterpillars start off crawling and get wings and become butterflies! Lark! You do not believe such nonsense yourself! You know it is impossible! Look at my long, green body and many legs, and then talk to me about having wings! Fool!"

"Oh, caterpillar," cried the indignant lark, "what comes from above I receive with trust."

"What do you mean by that?" asked the caterpillar. "On faith," answered the lark.

"How am I to learn faith?" asked the caterpillar. At that moment, she felt something at her side. She looked round to see eight or ten little green caterpillars were moving about who had already made a hole in the cabbage-leaf. They had broken out from the butterfly's eggs! Shame and amazement filled the green caterpillar's heart, but joy soon followed. For as the first wonder was possible, the second might be so too.

She had learned the lark's lesson of faith, and when she was going into her chrysalis, she said: "I shall be a butterfly some day!"

But her relations thought she was crazy and said, "Poor thing!"

The *Bhagavad Gita* says:

> The faith of each is in accordance with his nature,
> O Bharata. The man is made up of his faith; as a
> man's faith is, so is he.
>
> —Ch. 17, v. 3

He obtains wisdom who is full of faith, who is devoted to it, and who has subdued the senses. Having obtained wisdom, he ere long attains to the Supreme Peace.

—Ch. 4, v. 39

When our efforts and Amma's grace bear fruit, what will be our experience? Listen to the words of a *mahatma* who realized the Truth of his being.

"I am neither a man nor a god, neither a brahmachari, householder, nor sannyasi; I am pure Awareness alone.

"Just as the Sun causes all worldly movements, so do I—the ever-present, conscious Self—cause the mind to be active and the senses to function.

"Only those eyes that are helped by the Sun are capable of seeing objects, not others. The Source from which the Sun derives its power is my Self.

"Just as the reflection of the Sun on agitated waters seems to be broken up, but remains perfect on a calm surface, so also am I, the conscious Self, unrecognizable in agitated intellects though I clearly shine in those which are calm.

"Just as a transparent crystal takes on the color of its background, but is in no way changed thereby, and just as the unchanging moon on being reflected on undulating surfaces appears agitated, so is it with me, the all-pervading Supreme Reality."

—Hastamalaka Stotra

This is the experience of Self-Realization.

# CHAPTER FIVE

# Childlike Innocence Towards the Guru

Amma stresses a lot on the importance of childlike innocence in spiritual life. Christ also said a very similar thing:

"Unless you become as little children, you will by no means enter the Kingdom of Heaven. Whoever humbles himself as this little child is the greatest in the Kingdom of Heaven. Let the little children come to Me, and do not forbid them, for of such is the Kingdom of Heaven."

The Kingdom of Heaven is not a place above the clouds. It is the state of God-consciousness. It may also be an actual plane of existence where enlightened souls reside.

Try to remember when you were a child. What was the main difference between then and now? Children innocently believe anything and have no worries. They live in the present. Their negative feelings last only a moment. They are full of life and see everything around them as full of life. Their ideas about God are refreshing and innocent, to say the least.

### A Six-Year Old's Perception of God

"One of God's main jobs is making people. He makes these to put in the place of the ones who die so there will be enough people to take care of things here on earth. He doesn't make grownups; he just makes babies. I think because they are smaller and easier to make. That way he doesn't have to take up his valuable time teaching them to walk and talk. He can just leave that up to the mothers and fathers. I think it works out pretty good.

"God's second most important job is listening to prayers. An awful lot of this goes on, 'cause some people, like preachers and things, pray other times besides bedtimes, and Grandpa and Grandma pray every time they eat, except for snacks. God doesn't have time to listen to the radio or watch TV on account of this. 'Cause God hears everything, there must be a terrible lot of noise in his ears unless he has thought of a way to turn it down.

"God sees and hears everything and is everywhere, which keeps him pretty busy. So you shouldn't go wasting his time asking for things that aren't important, or go over parents' heads and ask for something they said you couldn't have. It doesn't work anyway."

—The Joyful Newsletter

When we come to a Self-realized master like Amma, she will put a lot of effort into revealing our innocent side. How does one become innocent? It is not that we do not have it. It is there, but hidden under the façade of anger, pride, lust, ambition and other "grown up" traits. These traits have to be removed in order for innocence to shine. The sun is always there, even on the cloudiest day. Innocence is our true nature; we are really children of God, but we have become children of "man" inadvertently. Amma's life is about awakening us to our true nature. In fact, just by spending some time with her, we gain in innocence. Her presence is like the sun, which dries up moisture. It dries up our negative nature to bring forth our "inner child." We experience relief and a refreshing feeling when we are with her.

Amma knows that being with her is only the beginning of regaining our innocence. She will personally work on us when we are physically with her, and even away from her. Our life will become such as to purify our minds from those qualities that cover it. We have swallowed the poison of negativity. It must be vomited out in order for purity to shine. It we want someone to vomit, we make them drink a lot of salt water or stick a finger down their throat. Similarly, Amma will bring about situations in our life that will bring out the worst in us, so that the best can shine afterwards. We may feel as if after meeting her, our anger, lust, pride or bad luck has increased so much.

We thought that we would get more and more blissful in our association with Amma as the days go by, but what has happened? When we vomit up something that is making us sick, we initially feel awful. Afterwards, we will recover. The stage of suffering that we go through by Amma's grace will be over some day and will give way to bliss. This is a spiritual principle: first suffering, then bliss. Like a mother holds her child's hand while he learns to walk, Amma will keep her omnipresent Eye of Wisdom on her children while they struggle to walk in the path of spiritual realization. She will do her duty towards us, but our faith should not falter.

Amma takes us to a state of uncharted territory. No one can say exactly what has been the path of a bird in the sky or a fish in the sea. Real spirituality is like that. The path is subtle and different for everyone. It is not in books and cannot be learned except through the grace of a mahatma. Essentially, it consists of surrender of the ego, the false sense of individuality, to God's and Guru's will. This will take us to the goal that the Master holds out to us.

Of course, this process may seem to be counter intuitive to us due to our modern upbringing. The present day culture teaches us to strengthen the personality more and more. One must wonder if this is truly the way to become peaceful and happy, since without peace there can be no happiness.

One way to conceive of this process is to consider oneself as a wave on the ocean. The ocean is God and the wave is a manifestation of the ocean. It is never separate from it but seems to have an individual existence. The depths of the ocean are calm, but the wave is in a constant state of movement and restlessness. If the wave could just sink beneath the surface, it would experience its oneness with the vast ocean and become it.

## A Test of the Guru

Bhai Gurudas was the uncle and devoted disciple of the Sikh Guru Arjan. At one time he composed the following couplets and read them to the Guru:

If a mother is impious, it is not for her son to punish her;

If a cow swallows a diamond, her stomach should not be cut open;

If a husband is unfaithful, the wife should never imitate him or lose her chastity;

If a high caste lady takes to wine, people should not take it ill;

If the Guru tests his disciple, the disciple's faith should not waver.

Guru Arjan listened attentively as Gurudas read. When he finished, the Guru thought, 'All these things are easier said than done. Let me test his faith.' Turning to Gurudas, he said, "Uncle, I have to buy some horses at Kabul. Will you be able to do this for me?"

"Why not? Certainly," replied Gurudas.

Accordingly, the Guru filled several bags with gold sovereigns. Gurudas counted them, and then sealed the bags and put them into strong wooden boxes. These were loaded onto the backs of mules and he, along with a number of disciples, started out on the long and arduous journey to Kabul from Lahore, where the Guru was residing. In due course, after passing through the Khyber Pass, they reached Kabul amongst the mountains of Hindu Kush.

In the great horse market of this ancient city, Gurudas bargained with the horse traders and finally purchased the best horses that he could find. These were taken by the other disciples, who were to take them slowly to Lahore. Meanwhile, Gurudas asked the horse traders to come to his tent to be paid. Leaving them outside, he entered the tent to get the gold.

Opening a few of the boxes, he took out the needed bags but felt that something was wrong. He opened all of the bags and, to his horror, found that every one of them was filled with pebbles instead of gold. He was now beside himself with fear, for he knew the savage nature of the horse dealers. 'There they are waiting outside the tent for me to pay them, and if I don't, they will cut me to pieces,' he thought. He taxed his brain and finally decided that the only way he might escape was to cut the back of the tent and escape through the hole. He did not even pray to his Guru for help; he was so full of terror. Jumping through the hole, he escaped and ran away at full speed. Ashamed to face his Guru, he passed through Lahore and made his way to Kashi, hundreds of miles to the east.

Meanwhile, the other members of his party entered his tent to find out why he was delaying in paying the horse dealers. There, they found all of the boxes open and filled with gold, but there was no sign of Gurudas. They also saw the hole in the back of the tent. They then paid the horse traders and made their way back to Lahore where they told Guru Arjan about all that had happened.

After Gurudas had settled down in Kashi, he started to expound the great truths of the scriptures in public places and soon attracted a large crowd. Finally, even the Governor of Kashi came to hear and admire his beautiful discourses.

After a few months, Guru Arjan sent a letter to the Governor of Kashi in which he wrote, "There is a thief of mine in Kashi, and I am writing to ask you to kindly take him prisoner, tie his hands and send him to me. You will not have to search hard for this thief. The mere reading of this letter in places of public assembly and religious discourses will find him, for the thief will himself speak out upon hearing the letter read."

In due course, the letter was read where Gurudas was giving a discourse to a large crowd of people. But the moment he heard the letter, he stood up and said, "I am the Guru's thief." His listeners were stunned.

"You could never be a thief, for you are a holy man. The thief must be someone else," they said.

But Gurudas insisted, "No, it is I who am the thief. There is no doubt about it. Please tie my hands so that I do not escape."

No one came forward to do so, for it was unthinkable to tie up a holy man like a common robber. So Gurudas unbound his turban and, cutting it in two, tied his own hands with it. Tied like this, he then happily made his way to Lahore.

When he finally reached there and stood before the Guru, the Guru said,

"Brother, please repeat those couplets you read to me just before I asked you to go to Kabul."

But Gurudas, having been tested and put through

some bitter experiences to try his love and faith, fell at the Guru's feet and exclaimed,

"If a mother gives poison to her son, who is it that will save him?

"If the watchman breaks into the house, who can protect it?

"If a guide misleads the traveler, who can set him on the right path?

"If the fence starts to eat the crop, who can save it?

"Even so, if the Guru tests the disciples, who can help them to remain steadfast?"

Only the *Satguru*, through her spiritual power and grace, can keep the disciple steadfast and filled with devotion under trying circumstances.

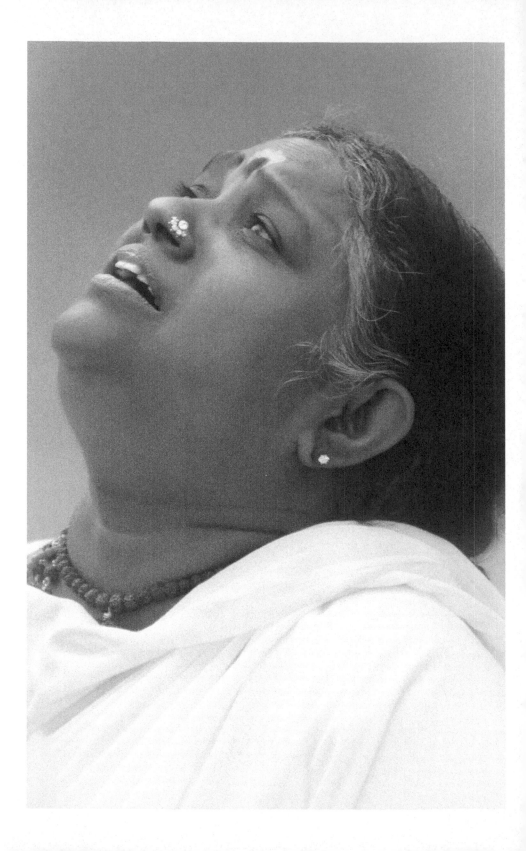

# CHAPTER SIX

## *Kindness vs Selfishness*

Amma says:

"Children, if you are desirous of attaining Liberation, give up selfishness. Try to listen to the sorrows of the afflicted."

Most of us do not know what is meant by "Liberation" in the sense that Amma is using it. Usually it means freedom or release from imprisonment, slavery, or oppression. Amma also means the same thing, but in the broadest sense of the word, to be free from all the limitations of individual existence. Our hands and feet may not be chained, we may not be locked up in jail or in a room, but our minds are bound to react with attraction, repulsion or fear, resulting in pleasure, pain or anxiety according to circumstances. Most of us have very little peace of mind, and the next moment may destroy what little we have. Our mind is restless like a monkey and has to be kept occupied every moment. Otherwise we feel bored or fall asleep.

Suppose we have invested a lot of money in the stock market. The Dow is going up and up and we are feeling happier and happier. We are in seventh heaven. Then the Federal Reserve breaks some bad news and the market falls, or perhaps our company's stock price tumbles or our competition overtakes us. Maybe our boss starts to harass us. Before we can remedy the situation, we have lost some of our fortune and peace of mind. We may become miserable and constantly worry. This happens all the time all around us, even though we think that it won't happen to us.

Many years ago, I knew a devotee who lost everything when the tech bubble burst. However, while some were committing suicide, this person was able to maintain an even mind due to their sadhana and years of association with Amma. It was a real example of the practical benefits of following Amma's teaching on surrender and detachment. It is strange that the average person does not learn such a technique from their parents or at school. This must be one reason why Amma says that there are two kinds of education: one to make a living and the other to know how to live.

Even trivial circumstances can upset many of us. We have all heard of road rage. Or maybe our wife or husband, our child or a friend keeps us waiting and fuming. We may yell at those who make us suffer even slightly. Life ends up being a hell for everyone—us and others who know us.

### A Story of The Secret of Heaven and Hell

An old Japanese monk sat by the side of the road in deep meditation with his eyes closed, his legs crossed and his hands folded in his lap. Suddenly, his meditation was interrupted by the harsh and demanding voice of a samurai warrior. "Old man! Teach me about heaven and hell!"

At first, there was no perceptible response from the monk as though he had not heard. But gradually he began to open his eyes, the faintest hint of a smile playing around the corners of his mouth as the samurai stood there, waiting impatiently, growing more and more agitated with each passing second.

"You wish to know the secrets of heaven and hell?" replied the monk at last. "You who are so unkempt; you whose hands and feet are covered with dirt; you whose hair is uncombed, whose breath is foul, whose sword is all rusty and neglected; you who are ugly and whose mother dresses you funny. You would ask me of heaven and hell?"

The samurai uttered a vile curse. He drew his sword and raised it high above his head. His face turned to crimson, and the veins on his neck stood out in bold relief as he prepared to sever the monk's head from its shoulders.

"That is hell," said the old monk gently, just as the sword began its descent.

In that fraction of a second, the samurai was overcome with amazement, awe, compassion and love for this gentle being who had dared to risk his very life to give him such a teaching. He stopped his sword in mid-flight and his eyes filled with grateful tears.

"And that," said the monk, "is heaven."

Because of Maya, God's Universal Power of Illusion, our mind looks out through the senses and makes us believe that happiness lies outside. We always try to satisfy our inner restlessness and urge for peace and happiness by adjusting our circumstances to yield the maximum amount of pleasure and then try to hold on to it. Unless we are a rare selfless type, we become selfish trying to preserve our happiness even at the cost of other's happiness. This is a very fragile kind of happiness and can collapse at any moment, evaporating with a change of luck.

We seem to have a certain amount of freedom, but many times, in spite of our efforts, most things don't go according to our wishes. Ultimately, as we get old or even before that, our health deteriorates and we die. When that time comes, no doctor can help us. Our bodies and minds are bound by the laws of Nature. It is not a very pleasant scenario. Life is full of limitations ending in death.

When Amma mentions attaining Liberation, she has in mind escaping the need for all the lifetimes we may have to experience if we don't purify our minds. The energy of our constant search for happiness propels us through numerous births until we become disillusioned by it all and turn our mind within to find our True Self, the source of happiness, and abide there forever. That is Liberation, liberation from the seemingly endless cycle of birth, death and rebirth, samsara. That is the sublime goal of this pilgrimage of life that all living beings are on.

Experiencing our Self not only requires of us to do various spiritual practices like mantra japa, meditation, devotional singing and scriptural study, but also to develop kindness, patience and compassion, in other words, selflessness. The ego or individual person whom we are mistakenly identifying with, gradually gets purified and expands to reveal our True Nature.

We think that by being selfish we will be happy, but we get just the opposite result again and again. This is the play of Maya. This selfish attitude closes the heart lotus. Everyone has a heart, not the blood-pumping organ but the place in the body where we feel happiness and misery. When it is closed and dark, we do not feel happiness or peace. When it opens a little, a bit of light creeps in, and we feel happy and peaceful. The more it opens, the more blissful and peaceful our life becomes. A fully blossomed heart lotus is the same as Self-realization. Negative thoughts and actions like anger, impatience, selfishness, revenge, etc., close it more and more. Positive thoughts such as affection, patience, selflessness, self-sacrifice, forgiveness and sharing open it. The great sage Patanjali advises us how to adjust our attitudes so that our heart stays open:

> By cultivating attitudes of friendliness toward the happy, compassion for the unhappy, delight in the virtuous, and disregard toward the wicked, the mind-stuff retains its undisturbed calmness.

> —Yoga Sutras of Patanjali, Ch.1, v.33

We can open it by doing good things, speaking good words and thinking good thoughts. We should not knowingly or unknowingly close it and suffer. Use the "open sesame" of goodness. This is very simple; not a hard philosophy to follow. Mahatmas are more pleased when we do good things, renouncing selfishness, than if we bring them flowers, clothes and fruits, or do *bhajan* (devotional singing) and meditation.

## A Story About Kindness

The Bible does not tell us how many wise men, or magi, journeyed to Bethlehem following the star at the time of Jesus' birth. Popular tradition holds that there were three—Caspar, Melchior and Balthazar. But there is also a tradition of a fourth wise man, named Artaban. As Artaban prepared to set out and follow the star, he took with him a sapphire, a ruby and a pearl of great value as gifts for the newborn king, wherever he was to be found.

On his way to join the other wise men, Artaban stopped to care for a sick traveler. However, if he stayed to help further, he would miss the rendezvous with his friends. He decided to stay, and the delay was just enough to make him late for the departure of the caravan. Now Artaban was alone, and he needed transportation and supplies to cross the desert. So he sold the sapphire to purchase camels and necessities, but he was saddened because the king would never have this precious gem.

Artaban journeyed onward and reached Bethlehem, but again, he was too late. There were soldiers everywhere carrying out Herod's command that all male children should be slain. Artaban, therefore, took out the brilliant ruby to bribe the captain and save the children in the village in which he was staying. Children were savedd and mothers rejoiced, but the ruby, also, would not reach the king.

For thirty-three years, Artaban searched in vain, and finally found his way to Jerusalem on the day several crucifixions were to take place. He hurried towards Calvary in order to bribe the Roman guard with the precious pearl and save the man called Jesus. Something told him that this was the King of kings for whom he had been searching all his life.

Just then, a young woman being dragged along the street toward the slave market, called out to Artaban, pleading for help. With only a slight hesitation, he gave the last jewel, the pearl of great price, for her ransom. Now Artaban had none of the precious gems he had been going to present to the king.

Reaching the place where the crucifixions were to occur, he felt heartbroken when he saw that he could do nothing to help Jesus. But then, something remarkable happened. Jesus looked toward Artaban and said to him,

"Don't be brokenhearted, Artaban. You've been helping me all your life. When I was hungry, you gave me food, when I was thirsty, you gave me drink, when I was naked, you clothed me, when I was a stranger, you took me in."

Some say Artaban never found Christ. Others say he was the wisest of the wise men. I am sure that Amma would agree with the latter.

To open the heart lotus is the most difficult and rewarding thing we can do. It strikes at the root of the ego, at selfishness. That is *tapas*, that is *sadhana*. Patiently listening to others who are suffering without feeling restless or bored, forgetting our little self for others' sake for comforting them, is the high path of selfless existence that Amma shows us every moment of the day and night. Can we follow her example even a little? Surely we can try.

# CHAPTER SEVEN

# Peace is Our True Nature

Everyone wants peace of mind. No matter how much sense enjoyment we may have, eventually we get tired and want only peace. A wealthy person may have all conceivable pleasures, but finally, even their most dear husband or wife, boyfriend or girlfriend, cannot keep them awake when they are tired and want to enjoy the bliss of sleep. What is it about sleep that makes it dearer than even sense enjoyment? Peace, the absence of subject and object, a blissful oneness.

If we persist in our efforts at sadhana and don't waste our energies in excessive sense enjoyment or thinking, then the mind will gradually calm down into a state of meditation. It will be calm even when one is not doing meditation. This calmness is the real beginning of spiritual life.

All spiritual efforts are followed only with the object of concentrating the restless mind. Peace is our true nature, not the different qualities of the mind like forgetting, remembering, desiring, hating, attracting and discarding. Not even spiritual powers, like knowing the past and future are our true nature. To know one's true nature as perfect peace and to remain as that is Liberation; that is the highest bliss and fulfillment.

Until this state of unceasing tranquility is attained, Amma says,

> "Make the mind starve. Stop feeding the mind with thoughts. We continue feeding the mind with the food of desires and thoughts. This has become a habit, and the mind now thinks that this is the best food. This is a habit that should be stopped. The mind should know that this food will give us a 'stomach ache,' if not now, then later. The mind should learn that this food of thoughts and desires is harmful and that there is food far tastier and healthier than this. The various spiritual practices make up the most delicious and healthful food. Once you experience this, you should feed the mind regularly with the Divine Name, *japa* (repeating a mantra), *dhyana* (meditation) and other spiritual practices. Slowly the hunger to have more and more of this spiritual food will grow until at last it becomes a terrible hunger.

> "Children, don't forget to chant your mantra. The period of sadhana is like climbing a high mountain. You need a lot of strength and energy. Mountain climbers use ropes for pulling themselves up. For you, the only rope is japa. Therefore, children, try

to repeat your mantra constantly. Once you reach the peak of God-Realization, you can relax and rest forever."

There are many ways to that sublime goal. Amma says,

"Each person is made differently. We are all unique. Although we talk of different means to peace of mind such as japa, prayer and meditation, there are many more. For some, it comes through art or music, dance or drama."

## A Song in the Heart, an Offering to God

Three neighborhood boys, Salvador, Julio and Antonio, lived and played in Cremona, Italy, around the mid-1600s.

Salvador had a beautiful tenor voice and Julio played the violin in accompaniment as they strolled through the town square. Antonio also liked music and would have loved to sing along, but his voice squeaked like a creaky door hinge. All the children made fun of him whenever he tried to sing. Yet Antonio was not without talent. His most prized possession was the pocketknife his grandfather had given him. He was always whittling away on some piece of wood. In fact, Antonio made some very nice things through his whittling.

As the time for the annual festival approached, the houses and streets gradually became festooned with beautiful decorations for spring. Dressed in their finest clothes, people filled the streets. One festival day, Salvador and Julio planned to go to the cathedral, where they would play and sing in the crowded plaza.

"Would you like to come with us?" they called to Antonio, who sat on his stoop whittling on a piece of wood. "Who cares if you can't sing. We'd like to have you come with us anyway."

"Sure, I'd like to come along," Antonio replied. "The festival is so much fun."

The three boys went off to the cathedral. As they walked along, Antonio kept thinking about their remark about his not being able to sing. It made him cry in his heart because he loved music as much as they did, even if his voice did squeak a little.

When they arrived at the plaza, Julio began to play the violin while Salvador sang with his melodious voice. People stopped to listen, and most of them left a coin or two for the shabbily dressed boys. An elderly man stepped out from the crowd. He complimented them and placed a shiny coin into Salvador's hand. He was quickly lost in the milling crowd.

Salvador opened his hand and gasped, "Look! It's a gold coin." He clenched it between his teeth to make sure. All three boys were excited and passed the coin back and forth, examining it. They all agreed that it was a real gold piece.

"But he can well afford it," said Julio. "You know, he's the great Amati."

Antonio asked sheepishly, "And who is Amati? Why is he so great?"

Both boys laughed as they said, "You've never heard of Amati?"

"Of course he hasn't," said Julio. "He knows nothing about music makers. He has a squeaky voice and is just a whittler of wood." Julio went on, "For your information, Antonio, Amati happens to be a great violin maker, probably the best in all of Italy or even the entire world, and he lives here in our city."

As Antonio walked home that evening, his heart was very heavy. It seemed that he had been laughed at too often for his squeaky voice and his whittling. So, very early the next morning, Antonio left his home, carrying his precious whittling knife. His pockets were stuffed with some of the things he had made—a pretty bird, a flute, several statues and a small boat. He was determined to find the home of the great Amati.

Eventually, Antonio found the house and gently knocked on the front door. When a servant opened it, the great master heard Antonio's squeaky voice and came to see what he wanted so early in the morning.

"I brought these for you to see, Sir," replied Antonio, as he emptied his pockets of the assortment of items that he had carved. "I hope you will look at these and tell me if I have enough talent to learn how to make violins, too."

Amati carefully picked up and examined each piece, and invited Antonio into his house. "What is your name?" he asked.

"Antonio, Sir" he squeaked.

"And why do you want to make violins?" inquired Amati, now quite serious.

Impulsively, Antonio blurted, "Because I love music, but I cannot sing as my voice sounds like a squeaky door hinge. You heard how well my friends sing yesterday in front of the cathedral. I, too, want to make music come alive."

Leaning forward and looking Antonio in the eyes, Amati said, "The thing that matters most is the song in the heart. There are many ways of making music—some people play the violin, others sing, still others paint wonderful pictures. Each helps to add to the splendor of the world. You are a whittler, but your song shall be as noble as any."

These words made Antonio very happy, and he never forgot this message of hope. In a very short while, Antonio became a student of the great artist. Very early every morning, he went to Amati's workshop, where he listened and learned and watched his teacher. After many years there was not one secret about the making of a violin, with all of its seventy different parts, that he did not know. By the time he was twenty-two years old, his master allowed him to put his own name on a violin he had made.

For the rest of his life, Antonio Stradivari made violins—more than 1,100 of them—trying to make each one better and more beautiful than the one before. Today anyone who owns a Stradivarius violin owns a treasure, a masterpiece of art worth millions of dollars.

We may not be great spiritual aspirants or perfect renunciates, but we can offer whatever we can to God and He will be pleased.

As Lord Krishna says in the *Bhagavad Gita*,

> "When one offers to Me with devotion a leaf, a flower, a fruit, water,—that I eat, offered with devotion by the pure-minded. Whatever you do, whatever you eat, whatever you sacrifice, whatever you give, in whatever austerity you engage, do it as an offering to Me. Thus shall you be liberated and shall come to Me."

—Ch. 9, v. 26

CHAPTER EIGHT

# The Unique Purpose
# of Human Birth

Amma does not mince words about the seriousness of life and the value of human birth. It is only after many, many births in lower forms of life that the soul gets a human form. In every birth including the human one, we are primarily concerned with the following four things: hunger and thirst, sex, fear, sleep.

So what is so special in being human? We can reason things out for the long term and make decisions in accordance with our conclusions and act accordingly. Animals cannot do that. They are programmed by Nature or can be trained by man, but they cannot think and reason like man. Humans have an intellect that can discriminate between what is good and what is bad and can understand many things. This trademark of humanity must be exercised to its fullest capacity before death. This does not necessarily mean developing the intellect's worldly knowledge. It means the realization of our eternal nature as a soul, as consciousness. Self-Knowledge is the highest achievement, the greatest happiness of birth as a human. Only humans have the capacity to make effort towards transcending Nature through spiritual practice and control of our instincts.

Amma:

> "Children, these bodies of ours are not eternal. They can perish at any moment. We are born as human beings after countless other births. If we waste this life living like animals, we will have to be born again as animals before attaining another human birth."

Some present day spiritual people argue that the teaching of the ancient sages or *rishis* stating that a human can be reborn as a subhuman cannot be true. It just sounds too unpleasant! Yet, the rishis and holy books like the Bhagavad Gita have told us that, in the long journey that the soul or *jiva* passes through on its way to mystical Union with the Creator, it may take many diversions leading to births both lower as well as higher than the human.

By having a clear conception of the goal of human existence along with an 'action plan' or 'flow chart,' one's life can have a definite direction and become fruitful. Even if the goal is not reached by the end of one's life, one will get a more conducive birth next time. This is clearly stated in an enlightening discussion between Lord Sri Krishna and His devotee Arjuna in the Bhagavad Gita, 6th chapter, which we should attentively read.

Arjuna said:

This Yoga in equanimity, taught by Thee, O Destroyer of Madhu, I see not its steady continuance, because of the restlessness (of the mind). The mind verily is, O Krishna, restless, turbulent, strong and obstinate. Thereof the restraint I deem quite as difficult as that of the wind.

The Blessed Lord said:

Doubtless, O mighty-armed, the mind is hard to restrain and restless; but by practice, O son of Kunti, and by indifference it may be restrained. Yoga, methinks is hard to attain for a man of uncontrolled self; but by him who (often) strives, self-controlled, it can be acquired by (proper) means.

Arjuna said:

He who strives not, but who is possessed of faith, whose mind wanders away from Yoga, having failed to attain perfection in Yoga, what end, O Krishna, does he meet? Having failed in both, does he not perish like a riven cloud, supportless, O mighty-armed, and perplexed in the path to Brahman? This doubt of mine, O Krishna, do Thou dispel completely; for none other than Thyself can possibly destroy this doubt.

The Blessed Lord said:

O Partha, neither in this world nor in the next is there destruction for him; none verily, who does good, My son, ever comes to grief. Having attained to the worlds of the righteous and having dwelt there for eternal years, he who failed in yoga is reborn in a house of the pure and wealthy. Else, he is born in a family of wise Yogins only. A birth like this is very hard to obtain in this world. There he regains touch with the knowledge that was acquired in the former body and strives more than before for Perfection, O son of the Kurus. By that very former practice is he borne on, though unwilling. Even he who merely wishes to know of Yoga rises superior to the Word-Brahman. Verily, a Yogin who strives with assiduity, purified from sins and perfected in the course of many births, then reaches the Supreme Goal.

—v. 33-45

These verses give us great hope and comfort during our spiritual life. When we devotees look at our present state, it is natural to feel that we may not reach the goal in this lifetime. We worry about our fate and what our next birth will be like. Will all our effort be for nothing? Will we have to start all over from scratch? Sri Bhagavan tells us not to worry. Nothing goes to waste. Our efforts are like putting money into an eternal bank account that survives our death, life after life. We will be happy in the other worlds and be reborn in circumstances that will be conducive to our further spiritual evolution. And even though unwilling, we will continue with more intensity towards the goal.

The use of the word 'unwilling' is very informative. Maya is like gravity. It is always pulling us down even though we are not aware of it except in certain circumstances. Due to Maya, souls in this world do not normally feel attracted to serious spiritual endeavor. Almost all beings get engaged in the satisfaction of their latent desires for pleasure and for avoiding suffering. But those who sincerely struggled for Liberation in their previous lifetimes will, in spite of their worldly tendencies, be drawn to make further and stronger efforts towards Self-realization. Amma says that the very fact that someone is making relatively quick spiritual progress means that they had done sadhana in their previous life. Their intensity in this life belies that fact. Even if we do not have such intensity, we should make efforts now so that, even if we don't reach the Supreme State in this life, we will be that much closer in the next life. It is a wise investment.

Apart from these words of assurance, we should not forget that our Guru's grace is the most powerful force for Liberation. Amma's mere thought directed towards us is enough to tear away the ancient veil of spiritual ignorance or *ajñana* that hides our True Self. Of course, we must invoke that grace through our own intense efforts.

### The Plan for Children

So, what is the action plan? When we are children, we are only two-legged animals. We do nothing other than what animals do: eat, excrete, sleep, play, love, fight, etc. But then, after a little while, after the age of five or so, our parents should start to build the foundation for our 'tower to heaven.' In this stage, the provisions that we are going to need to make the long journey back to God must be procured.

> Amma: "Parents should start explaining spiritual ideas to children at an early age. We should tell them that there is a power known as God who controls everything. If we teach a child to remember this Divinity in all circumstances of life, that child will be able to keep his or her inner poise in every situation, whether it be victory or defeat. Even if they acquire bad habits when they grow up, the good impressions dormant in their subconscious mind will bring them back to the right path in due course."

Apart from worldly knowledge, parents should expose their children to the following subjects through examples and stories: reverence towards elders and God, worship, humility, simplicity, self-control, detachment, service, selflessness and a philosophic attitude.

Amma: "Children should respect their elders, answering them politely, obeying their instructions, refraining from making fun of them or answering them loudly or in a contrary way. These qualities are all essential for the welfare of the family."

For this to happen, children are to be taught the following: yoga asanas, Sanskrit slokas and prayers, spiritual stories from *Ramayana, Bhagavata, Mahabharata or Panchatantra, bhajans*, meditation and *japa*, and engaging in *karma yoga* or *seva*. These are in addition to their secular studies. All these practices will form a foundation for a spiritual life at some time later on.

## Married Life

Most of us have desires for a spouse, wealth and fame, comforts and possessions, sense pleasures and children. These things are fulfilled in married life. However, the spiritual practices that we learned as children should be continued in this stage also. Passions like anger, greed, selfishness, jealousy and sexual desire are to be gradually controlled, gradually reduced. Gradually is the word here, but not so gradual that nothing is done about it! Married life is a stage where there are plenty of opportunities for self-improvement. It is unfortunate that, when we look around, we don't see much of these positive qualities in people's lives today. Selfishness seems to rule the roost!

### In the Forest

If one has worked hard at purifying the mind of all its weaknesses and negativities and been regular in spiritual practice, then real devotion and detachment should arise. One is then ready for 'residence in the woods.' This is the stage of living a life unconcerned with worldly affairs, and if possible, settling down in an ashram or at least spending all one's time in spiritual practices at home.

> Amma: "Once the children are grown up and are able to take care of themselves, husband and wife should go to an ashram and lead a spiritual life, working for their spiritual improvement by engaging in meditation, japa and selfless service. It is necessary to cultivate from the beginning of one's spiritual life an attitude of strong attachment only to the Lord in order to make this transition possible. Without such a spiritual bond, the mind will cling to its ties; first to the children, then to the grandchildren and so on. This kind of clinging is of no use to us or our children. Our lives will be a waste if we allow our clinging to persist! If, on the other hand, we spend our lives in sadhana, then our spiritual power will help both us and the world. Therefore, cultivate the habit of withdrawing the mind from the countless worldly subjects and turn it totally towards God. By collecting water in a storage tank, it can reach all the faucets equally. Likewise, by keeping our mind

on God constantly, while engaged in any work, the benefit will reach all members of the family. The ultimate aim in life should not be to amass wealth for children and relatives; it should be to focus on our own spiritual development."

## Renunciation

When one is convinced of the reality of God and the illusory nature of the world, when one's thirst for sense life is reduced only to survival, when one is burning for God-Realization, then comes the stage of complete renunciation, total dependence on God and complete dedication to spirituality. This may be an inner attitude or take the form of external renunciation as well. One's practice is to live in the Atman or soul. That is one's only real duty.

We should not think that only renunciates receive the grace of God or Guru. Grace comes in different forms according to our stage and practice. A married person may work for it and receive it in a different way than a monk.

## God's Hidden Servants

There is a legend about a hermit who lived long ago high up on a mountainside in a tiny cave. His food was roots and acorns, a bit of bread given by a peasant, or cheese brought by a woman who wanted his prayers; his work was praying, and thinking about God. For forty years he lived there, preaching to the people, praying for them, comforting those in trouble and, most of all, worshipping in his heart. There was just one thing he cared about: it was to make his soul so pure and perfect that it could be one of the stones in God's great Temple of Heaven.

One day, after the forty years, he had a great longing to know how much progress he had made with his work, how it looked to God. He prayed that he might be shown a man—

> "Whose soul in heavenly grace had grown
> To the selfsame measure as his own;
> Whose treasure on the celestial shore
> Could neither be less than his nor more."

As he looked up from his prayer, a white-robed angel stood in the path before him. The hermit bowed before the messenger with great happiness, for he knew that his wish was answered.

"Go to the nearest town," the angel said, "and there, in the public square, you will find a clown making the people laugh for money. He is the man you seek, his soul has grown to the selfsame stature as your own; his treasure on the celestial shore is neither less than yours nor more."

When the angel had faded from sight, the hermit bowed his head again, but this time with great sorrow and fear. Had his forty years of prayer been a terrible mistake, and was his soul indeed like a clown, fooling around in the market-place? He knew not what to think. He almost hoped he should not find the man and could believe that he had dreamed the angel vision. But when he came to the village and the square, after a long, exhausting walk, alas, there was the clown, doing his silly tricks for the crowd.

The hermit stood and looked at him with terror and sadness, for he felt that he was looking at his own soul. The face he saw was thin and tired, and though it kept a smile or a grin for the people, it seemed very sad to the hermit. Soon, the man felt the hermit's eyes; he could not go on with his tricks. And when he had stopped and the crowd had left, the hermit went and drew the man aside to a place where they could rest; for he wanted more than anything else on earth to know what the man's soul was like, because what it was, his was. So, after a little, he asked the clown, very gently, what his life was, what it had been. And the clown answered, very sadly, that it was just as it looked—a life of foolish tricks, for that was the only way of earning his bread that he knew.

"But have you never been anything different?" asked the hermit, painfully.

The clown's head sank in his hands. "Yes, holy father," he said, "I have been something else. I was a thief! I once belonged to the wickedest band of mountain robbers that ever tormented the land, and I was as wicked as the worst."

Alas! The hermit felt that his heart was breaking. Was this how he looked to the Lord— like a thief, a cruel mountain robber? He could hardly speak, and the tears streamed from his old eyes, but he gathered strength to ask one more question. "I beg you," he said, "if you have ever done a single good deed in your life, remember it now, and tell it to me," for he thought that even one good deed would save him from utter despair.

"Yes, one," the clown said, "but it was so small, it is not worth telling; my life has been worthless."

"Tell me!" pleaded the hermit.

"Once," said the man, "our band broke into a convent garden and kidnapped one of the nuns to sell as a slave or to keep for a ransom. We dragged her with us over the rough, long way to our mountain camp, and set a guard over her for the night. The poor thing prayed to us so piteously to let her go! And as she begged, she looked from one hard face to another with trusting, imploring eyes, as if she could not believe men could be really bad. Father, when her eyes met mine something pierced my heart! Pity and shame leaped up, for the first time, within me. But I made my face as hard and cruel as the rest, and she turned away, hopeless.

"When all was dark and still, I stole like a cat to where she lay bound. I put my hand on her wrist and whispered, 'Trust me, and I will take you safely home.' I cut her bonds with my knife, and she looked at me to show that she trusted. Father, by terrible ways that I knew, hidden from the others, I took her safely to the convent gate. She knocked, they opened and she slipped inside. And, as she left me, she turned and said, 'God will remember.'

"That was all. I could not go back to the old bad life, and I had never learned an honest way to earn my bread. So I became a clown and must be a clown until I die."

"No! No! my son," cried the hermit, and now his tears were tears of joy. "God has remembered; your soul is in his sight even as mine, who have prayed and preached for forty years. Your treasure waits for you on the heavenly shore just as mine does."

"As yours? Father, you mock me!" said the clown.

But when the hermit told him the story of his prayer and the angel's answer, the poor clown was transfigured with joy, for he knew that his sins were forgiven. And when the hermit went home to his mountain, the clown went with him. He, too, became a hermit and spent his time in praise and prayer.

Together they lived and worked and helped the poor. And when, after two years, the man who had been a clown died, the hermit felt that he had lost a brother holier than himself.

For ten years more, the hermit lived in his mountain hut, thinking always of God, fasting and praying, and doing nothing that was wrong. Then, one day, the wish to know how his work was growing once more came, and once more, and he prayed that he might see a being like himself.

Once more, his prayer was answered. The angel came to him and told him to go to a certain village on the other side of the mountain to a small farm where two women lived. In them he would find two souls like his own, in God's sight.

When the hermit came to the gate of the little farm, the two women who lived there were overjoyed to see him, for everyone loved and honored his name. They put a chair for him on the cool porch and brought food and drink. But the hermit was too eager to wait. He longed greatly to know what the souls of the two women were like and, from their looks, he could see only that they were gentle and honest. One was old, and the other of middle age.

Presently, he asked them about their lives. They told him what little there was to tell: they had worked hard always, in the fields with their husbands, or in the house;

they had many children; they had seen hard times— sickness, sorrow, but they had never despaired.

"But what of your good deeds?" the hermit asked. "What have you done for God?"

"Very little," they said sadly, for they were too poor to give much. To be sure, twice every year, when they killed a sheep for food, they gave half to their poorer neighbors.

"That is very good, very faithful," the hermit said. "And is there any other good deed you have done?"

"Nothing," said the older woman, "unless, unless—it might be called a good deed…" She looked at the younger woman, who smiled back at her.

"What?" said the hermit.

Still, the woman hesitated; but at last she said, timidly, "It is not much to tell, Father, only this: that it is twenty years since my sister-in-law and I came to live together in the house; we have brought up our families here, and in all the twenty years there has never been a cross word between us, or a look that was less than kind."

The hermit bent his head before the two women, and gave thanks in his heart. "If my soul is as these," he said, "I am blessed indeed."

And, suddenly, a great light came into the hermit's mind, and he saw how many ways there are of serving God. Some serve him in ashrams, temples and in hermit's cells by praise and prayer; some poor souls, who have been very wicked, turn from their wickedness with sorrow and serve him with repentance; some live faithfully and gently in humble homes, working, bringing up children, keeping kind and cheerful; some bear pain patiently, for His sake. Endless, endless ways there are that only the Heavenly Being sees.

And so, as the hermit climbed the mountain again, he thought, as he saw the star-like glow of light in the cottage windows afar, 'How many of God's hidden servants there are!'

# CHAPTER NINE

# The Need for Renunciation

*Na karmana na prajaya dhanena*
*tyagenaike amrita tvamanasuh*
*parena nakam nihitam guhayam*
*vibhrajate yadyatayo visanti*

Neither by actions, nor by (acquiring) progeny
and wealth, but by renunciation alone is immortality attained. That Supreme State is far beyond
the highest heaven, and the sages perceive it,
hidden in the cave of the heart, shining brilliantly
therein.

—Mahanarayanopanisad 4.12

Amma speaks frequently about the value and necessity of renunciation. We generally don't think of renunciation as a means to happiness. It almost seems like a kind of torture, punishment or suffering to us, a real downer. But Amma says that the value in it lies in the lasting happiness it gives. Most of us feel that happiness is in whatever gives our mind and senses a feeling of pleasure. There is some truth in that. But Amma says that we need not settle for such limited and changing happiness. Why not strive for a pleasure that results in permanent satisfaction? Why run only after drops of honey when a whole ocean of it is available? This is what all wise people of all the ancient spiritual traditions say, born out of their own experience of union with God: There is an ocean of bliss within you. You are not aware of it now. Seek to experience it through spiritual practice and happiness and peace will be yours, a happiness that no one and no situation can take from you.

There are different degrees of *ananda* or happiness. There is human pleasure, there are the higher pleasures of the subtle or heavenly worlds, and then there is Divine Bliss or *Brahmananda*. Only Brahmananda lasts forever and is supreme in every respect. Attaining that, one rests content. A bird may fly around for any amount of time. Some birds can fly thousands of miles without resting, but eventually, they must come back to the earth. Similarly, we may wander about Creation over the course of many births searching for bliss but, eventually, we must come back home—we must land on the terra firma of our own source, the *Atman* or God.

What Amma means by renunciation is a gradual withdrawal of the mind and senses from worldly objects and fixing the attention on God, the unchanging Reality of this ever-changing world, the Divine Bliss, the Source of our mind. God is not a stodgy old man with a white beard, who lives in heaven and is always ready to punish us, keeping His finger on a "smite" button. God is the essence of Bliss, an infinitely vast Ocean of Awareness behind our individual minds.

Renunciation also means giving up that which is harmful to us spiritually. In an effort to do so, we come to see that our whole life, our upbringing and daily existence, have taught us to do just the opposite. In the course of following the ways of worldly happiness, we develop a great deal of negative or destructive tendencies like pride, selfishness, anger, impatience and greed. We employ these tendencies in making us happy, but in fact, they end up making us, and others, miserable. This is the strange working of *Maya*, the Power of Universal Illusion.

Renunciation is not something that most people can practice suddenly in a whole-hearted way. It should be gradually developed. Some married devotees have a feeling of guilt that they are striving for worldly goals and enjoying the pleasures of life even though Amma stresses renunciation. Yet Amma says that a *grihastashrami* or householder should enjoy what the world has to offer. Initially, try to be as fulfilled as possible through worldly life. Then, after some time, slowly and gradually practice renunciation. Eventually, try to see and understand the negative side of pleasure while at the same time developing devotion. We can do this through the company of *mahatmas* (great souls) and reading of traditional books such as Bhagavad Gita and Srimad Bhagavatam. Think about what the real goal of human life is. True renunciation is achieved only when the mind lives in God-consciousness.

Physical renunciation is not for everyone. It becomes possible for some in the fullness of time. Can anybody force himself into renunciation? A strong feeling of detachment from everyone and everything should first dawn on the devotee. Worldly pleasures and associations will feel empty and meaningless, a distraction and a waste of valuable time and life. Insight into worldly life's shallowness and selfishness should arise. The worldly environment will feel unbearable and empty, like a deep abyss. The attainment of Divine Bliss and escape from the cycle of death and rebirth will have a sense of urgency and become the foremost goals of one's life.

Some people embrace renunciation in a fit of disgust towards the pains, disappointments, and the hassles of worldly life. They may even leave their family and job and move to a holy place or one of natural beauty, or go on a pilgrimage; but sooner or later, they may begin to miss their old life and return home. They may even start a new worldly life in a new setting.

There is another kind of renunciation called *smasana vairagya* (graveyard detachment). This happens when someone attends a cremation or funeral, sees a dead body or a horrific accident, or has a close brush with death. One starts to think that one's own body will someday be reduced to the same fate. One will become more philosophical about life and feel some detachment towards daily affairs, thus making one seriously consider spiritual effort. However, after reaching home and getting back into one's usual routine, such feelings are all forgotten.

In the case of Amma's devotees, she is there to decide whether or not we are fit for a life of renunciation. She can see beyond what we can see. The best course is for us to consult her about such matters. It is very difficult for us to truly know if we have enough detachment to lead such a life. Amma will show us the way and let us know if any adjustments need to be made.

### A Swami Who Loved Pudding

A swami had entered into the life of renunciation without getting the blessings of a Guru. He was living on fruits and roots in a hut in a forest retreat. His ashram was located near a village, and so the village children used to come frequently there to play. One day, he heard the children shouting and fighting, and came out to see what the matter was. Two brothers were fighting about the previous day's incident, where the elder boy did not share his sweet pudding (*payasam*) with the younger brother. Hearing the word 'payasam,' the desire to eat payasam arose in the sadhu's mind. His mind flew back to thirty years previous, when he still had lived with his family and regularly eaten payasam and anything else he desired.

He thought, 'How can I get payasam now? It would not be proper for me to go back to my house after so many years. I may get entrapped in the life there and many complications will develop. Well, there will not be any harm if I just wander around the village begging from a few houses. Maybe there will be payasam in one of them and I will get some.'

All these years the sadhu had been living off the produce of the forest so as to avoid the villagers. Now, he decided to go to the village. He left in the evening but got lost on the way. He had to wander around in the forest until the next morning. He finally heard some voices and went over to the spot. He asked them the way to the village, but was surprised to see their reaction.

"Here is the very thief that we have been looking for! He has disguised himself as a sadhu. Catch him!"

Grabbing hold of him, they beat him up and took him to the police station. The police threatened him with torture if he did not say where he had kept the stolen goods. The entire village came to see the thief dressed as a sadhu.

The sadhu was trembling with fear and was praying to God to save him. He had no idea what was happening.

Just then, a mahatma walked by on his way back from the river after a bath. He immediately understood the situation and told the policemen, "You have the wrong man. This man is only an innocent sadhu who lives in the forest about ten miles from here. The real thief has been caught somewhere else and is being held in custody. Please release this man, feed him some payasam, and send him back to his ashram."

The townspeople knew the mahatma well and therefore released the sadhu. The sadhu prostrated at the feet of the mahatma and burst into tears. He repented for his lack of control and returned to his hut in the forest. Desires always lead to trouble, especially in the case of a sadhu or renunciate who doesn't have a Guru!

Life in this world is like going to a school. We pass through different classes and learn different lessons. But this world is only a school. We should not stay here forever. We should try to graduate to the real world. That real world is the world of Divine Bliss, the world of God. Let us practice renunciation in whatever way and degree possible in our day-to-day life in accordance with Amma's advice. Even if we leave our home, the same mind will go with us. We can never escape it except through renunciation of thoughts.

# CHAPTER TEN

# *Vasanas*

Amma explains that the real goal of birth as a human being is to experience the state of union with our Creator, God, in a mind purified by spiritual discipline. In order for that experience to dawn on us, our present restless mind has to be purified of its thoughts and feelings and become as calm as a waveless ocean. In that process of purification, a *sadhak* (aspirant) tries to reduce thoughts so that the hidden Truth will become revealed. A pond may be covered by algae, but if you move the algae aside, you can see the water. Similarly, the Atma is now covered by thoughts, weak and strong. The vision or experience of the Self will start to be gained when the thoughts are reduced.

Amma says,

> "When mantras are chanted sincerely and with devotion, peace of mind and tranquility can be gained. This will decrease the number of thoughts. When there are fewer thoughts, you will get more peace of mind. Tension and mental agitation are caused by the numerous thought waves, which in turn bring forth all kinds of negative tendencies such as lust,

anger, jealousy, greed, etc. Mantras, when chanted with concentration, will enable us to accept both the pleasant and painful experiences of life as God's Will and blessing. This is not possible if your prayers are only to fulfill desires. That will only help to increase your sorrows and disappointments in life. Peace of mind is the most important thing."

In order to successfully reduce thoughts, we should become acutely aware of our mind through meditation. This focuses our attention within on the mind instead of on external affairs. The mind is made of the usual low-level noise or chatter and also very powerful feelings and thoughts, which can motivate us to action and create happiness or misery for us. They are the threads that make the cloth of the mind. These are the *vasanas* or habitual thoughts. Powered by these, we speak and act, getting immersed in the ocean of karma, pleasant or painful.

## The Three Gunas

Some thoughts and feelings are helpful to calm the mind and others will only agitate it. Those that calm it are sattvic, and those that distract it and cause us to suffer are rajasic and tamasic. These are the three *gunas* (qualities) that make up the Universe.

Lord Krishna says,

"When at every gate in this body there shoots up wisdom-light, then it may be known that *sattva* is predominant.

"Greed, activity, the undertaking of works, unrest, desire - these arise when *rajas* is predominant, O lord of the Bharatas.

"Darkness, heedlessness, inertness, and error, - these arise when *tamas* is predominant, O descendant of Kuru.

"If the embodied one meets death when sattva is predominant, then he attains to the spotless regions of the knowers of the Highest.

"Meeting death in rajas, he is born among those attached to action; and, dying in tamas, he is born in the wombs of the irrational.

"The fruit of good action, they say, is sattvic and pure; while the fruit of rajas is pain, and ignorance is the fruit of tamas.

"From sattva arises wisdom, and greed from rajas; heedlessness and error arise from tamas, and also ignorance.

"Those who follow sattva go upwards; the rajasic remain in the middle; and the tamasic, who follow in the course of the lowest guna, go downwards.

"Having crossed beyond these three gunas, which are the source of the body, the embodied one is freed from birth, death, decay and pain, and attains the Immortal."

—Bhagavad Gita, Ch.14, v.11-18, 20

Here, below, is an exhaustive list of qualities that manifest from the three gunas. By becoming familiar with it, we can understand where we are guna-wise and where we have to go.

Sattva: Patience, joy, satisfaction, purity, contentment, faith, liberality, forgiveness, firmness, benevolence, equanimity, truth, mildness, modesty, calmness, simplicity, dispassion, fearlessness, regard for the interests of others, and compassion for all creatures.

Rajas: Pride of personal beauty, assertion of power, war, stinginess, absence of compassion, being buffeted by happiness and misery, pleasure in speaking ill of others, indulgence in quarrels and disputes, arrogance, rudeness, anxiety, indulgence in hostilities, sorrow, appropriation of what belongs to others, shamelessness, crookedness, roughness, lust, wrath, pride, assertion of superiority, viciousness, and slandering others.

Tamas: heedlessness, indolence and sloth, inertness and error, unsteadiness, vulgarity, stubborness, deceptiveness, wickedness, indolence, procrastination.

Tamas can be overcome through rajas, which in turn can be sublimated through sattva. We must calm the mind down to such an extent that there are no qualities at all, only awareness, consciousness, bliss. But, as the Lord says,

"Verily this Divine Illusion of Mine, made up of gunas, is hard to surmount. Whoever seek Me alone, they cross over this Illusion."

—Bhagavad Gita, Ch. 7, v. 4.

This is very hard work. This struggle for mental purity is called *tapas* or austerity. There is no other way. Every living being must go through this struggle sooner or later and thereby become strong enough to bring the mind completely under control. If we don't struggle to raise ourselves, our negative vasanas will devour us and bring us a lot of pain, birth after birth.

Let a man raise himself by himself, let him not lower himself; for, he alone is the friend of himself, he alone is the enemy of himself.

To him who has conquered himself by himself, his own self is the friend of himself, but to him who has not (conquered) himself, his own self stands in the place of an enemy like an (external) foe.

—Bhagavad Gita, Ch.6, v. 5-6

**Life of a Butterfly**

A student found a cocoon one day and brought it to his homeroom, which was in the biology lab. The teacher put it into an unused aquarium with a lamp to keep the cocoon warm. About a week went by, when a small opening began to appear on the underside of the cocoon. The students watched as it began to shake. Suddenly, tiny antennae emerged followed by the head and tiny front feet. The students would run back to the lab in between classes to check on the progress of the cocoon. By lunch time it had struggled to free its listless wings, the colors revealing that it was a monarch butterfly. It wiggled, shook, and struggled, but now it seemed to be stuck. Try as it might, the butterfly couldn't seem to force its body through the small opening in the cocoon.

Finally, one student decided to help the butterfly out of its difficulty. He took scissors from the table, snipped off the cocoon's restrictive covering, and out plopped an insect-like thing. The top half looked like a butterfly with droopy wings, the bottom half, which was just out of the cocoon, was large and swollen. But it could never fly with its stunted wings; it just crawled around the bottom of the aquarium dragging its wings and swollen body. Within a short time, it died.

The next day, the biology teacher explained that the butterfly's struggle to get through the tiny opening was necessary in order to force the fluids from the swollen body into the wings so that they would be strong enough to fly. Without the struggle, the wings never developed and the butterfly could not fly. Like the butterfly, without struggles, we also cannot develop spiritually.

A life dedicated to spirituality can be discouraging at times. Amma says not to just lay there after a fall. Get up and move forward. The fall is not so important; what is important is the continued effort to succeed.

## Thomas Edison's Experience

We have all heard of Thomas Edison's experience. He tried two thousand different materials in search of a filament for the light bulb. When none worked satisfactorily, his assistant complained, "All our work is in vain. We have learned nothing."

Edison replied very confidently, "Well, we have come a long way, and we have learned a lot. We now know that there are two thousand elements that we cannot use to make a good light bulb."

Amma says that only a Guru can completely remove our vasanas. This may mean that we can go only so far through our own efforts, and then the Guru must reveal the transcendent Truth to us through her grace, or that the Guru will bring out everything from the depths of our mind, to be seen and then dealt with. We must become conscious of everything that is there in order to clean our house. We must do a real deep cleaning of our mind. Most of us are quite blind as to what is in there. We can readily see other's faults or what we think are faults, but are blissfully unaware of our own. Christ said, "And why do you look at the speck in your brother's eye, but do not consider the block of wood in your own eye?"

How will the Guru do this? Amma says,

> "The Guru will create obstacles and sorrows for the disciple. The disciple should overcome all that through intense sadhana. Spirituality is not for idle people. The difficulties of the subtle level are hard compared to the sorrows of the external world. But, there is nothing to fear for one who dedicates one's life to a Satguru.

> "The Guru will test the disciple in different ways. Only one who is endowed with strong determination can withstand all those tests and proceed on the spiritual path. But once those tests are passed, the infinite Grace of the Guru will flow towards the disciple unimpeded. Whatever the Guru does is only for the spiritual progress of the disciple. It is absolutely impossible for him to act otherwise. Amma is talking about a Satguru, not everyone who declares himself as a Guru. A true spiritual master sometimes may even behave strangely. He may get angry at the disciple without any particular reason

and might scold him, blaming him for errors that he hasn't committed. But that seemingly strange behavior is not because the Guru is angry with the student. That is the Guru's method of teaching self-surrender, patience and acceptance."

There is seemingly no end to the waves of vasanas rising up. We can never satisfy them by indulging in them. They will only become more deep-rooted through repetition. A single line drawn on paper with a pencil can be easily removed with an eraser, but if the line is drawn many times over itself, erasing it will become more difficult. A certain amount of worldly enjoyment and experience will help satisfy our cravings and habits, but at the same time, we must remember that only self-control and discrimination between what is real and what only appears to be real (but is, in truth, one's fancies) will completely uproot them. The Guru may give the sincere disciple some scope to reduce his/her vasanas, but she knows when to put an end to it and make the disciple evolve further. Maya makes it impossible for us to truly understand our predicament.

## The Guru's Love

"Master, however much I try to restrain it, my mind wanders towards the enjoyments of this world. Often I think of leaving you without informing you. But my love for you prevents me from taking such an ungrateful step.

My Lord, what must I do? Please guide me," a devotee thus pleaded to his Guru. It was just a month since he had entered his Guru's ashram.

"Child, I too have been watching your keen, inner struggle. Deeply embedded desires are hard to conquer. Fear not. Go forth into the world. Lead the life of a house-holder for some time and satisfy the intense cravings of your mind. But all the time fix your mind on the Lotus Feet of the Lord. Never lose sight of your goal. Come back after ten years. Do not stay longer."

The devotee took leave of his Guru. He went to his hometown, married and settled down to family life. He had served his Guru, heart and soul, and had earned his Guru's grace. Success waited upon him. Soon he was one of the most prosperous men in the town, with a loving wife and lovely children.

Ten years rolled by.

A mendicant stood on the doorstep of the devotee's bungalow. Seeing his scruffy appearance, the children ran into the house in fright. His wife was showering abuses on the sadhu, who remained unmoved and wanted to see the master of the house. The woman's husband rec-ognized his Guru. In a dignified manner, he greeted his old Master and offered him a seat.

"Well, ten years are over. Have you been able to satisfy yourself yet?"

"I have enjoyed all that the world has to offer, Gurudev. I could have come away to rejoin the ashram, but how can I leave these little children uncared for? Please allow me to stay for a few more years, educate them and see that they are settled in life. Then I shall surely join you."

Ten more years rolled by.

This time, it was an aged man that greeted the sadhu. His wife had departed from the world. His sons were young men now with families of their own.

"My beloved Guru," he said, "it is true I have fulfilled my duties of a household life. All my children are now grown up and are prosperous in life. Yet they are young. They are immersed in the pleasures of the world. They have no sense of responsibility. Left to themselves, they might squander away all the hard-earned wealth of their father and then starve. I have to plan their family budget and guide their actions. Please allow me to remain here for a few more years till they grow up into full adulthood and assume the responsibilities of the household. Then I shall certainly come away and join the ashram."

Seven years rolled by after this.

The Guru returned to see his disciple.

A big dog was guarding the gate. He recognized it; it was the devotee. He went into the house to learn that he had passed away a couple of years back. Such was his attachment to the family that he took birth as a dog and guarded his house and his children. The Guru entered into the soul of the dog.

"Well now, my child, are you ready to follow me?"

"Surely a couple of years hence, my Guru," replied the dog. "My children are now at the peak of their good fortune and prosperity, but they have several jealous enemies. In a couple of years they will be free from fear and worry. Then I shall run to your ashram."

Ten more years elapsed.

The sadhu returned to the house. The dog too, had died. He saw through his intuitive vision that his disciple had assumed the form of a venomous cobra and was living under the house. The Guru decided that the time had come to deliver him from delusion.

"Brother," he spoke to the grandson, "there is a venomous cobra in the space under your house. It is a dangerous snake. Kindly have it removed from there. Please do not kill it. Give it a good beating, break its back and bring it to me."

Looking under the house, the young man was astonished to find that the sadhu's words were true. He gathered all the youngsters of the household and began to beat the cobra. As requested by the sadhu, they did not kill it, but injured it enough so that it was unable to move. The sadhu fondly caressed its head and then, throwing it around his shoulders, quietly took leave of the grandchildren. They, too, were extremely happy to be miraculously saved from the venomous creature.

On his way back to the ashram, the Guru spoke to the cobra: "Beloved child! No one has so far been able to satisfy his senses and mind. Cravings are insatiable. Before one disappears, a dozen others crop up. Discrimination is your only refuge. Wake up! At least in your next birth you should attain the Supreme Reality."

"Gurudev" he cried bitterly. "How gracious you are! Even though I proved ungrateful to you, you have always graciously followed me and, never losing sight of me, have guided me back to your lotus feet. Surely there is none in the whole world who is as full of divine love as a Guru. There is no selfless love in the world except between a true Guru and his disciple."

The real Guru is God. He is within us in all our births and manifests as the Teacher when we are ready to come back to our Source. The Guru will draw us to Himself and develop a deep and lasting relationship. But this relationship is different than the relationship between two people. It is a relationship between God and the soul. He will bring about the sincere disciple's transformation one way or another and, putting an end to its wandering, awaken it to its True Nature as Pure Awareness.

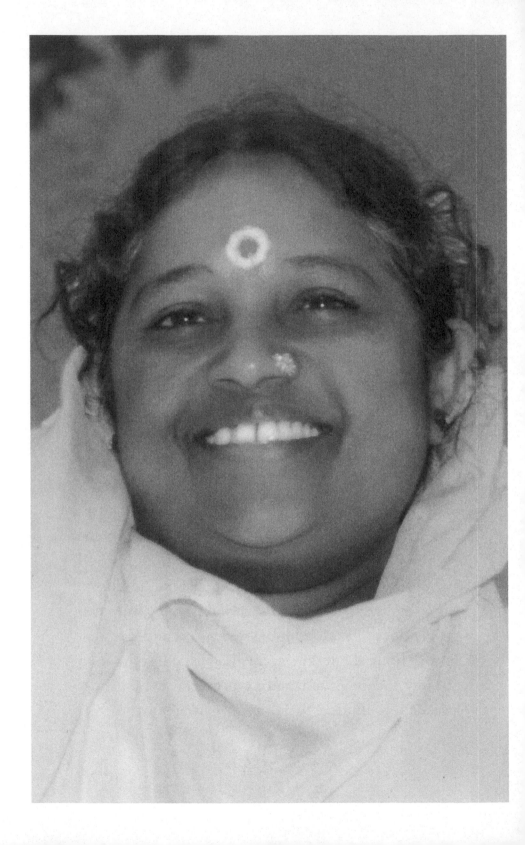

# CHAPTER ELEVEN

# Witnessing

Great people like Amma tell us that we should use our mind intelligently, not only to better our worldly affairs, but also to reach far beyond our present animal state to the state of Divinity, the state beyond the ordinary thinking mind. Amma says that mankind is capable of experiencing permanent peace of mind, eternal bliss, perfect contentment, and oneness with the Universal Cause—*Satchidananda Brahman* or God. We are not all only children of God but are manifestations of That. We are like waves on the surface of the ocean, which is their source and support. When the wave sinks into the ocean, it becomes the ocean itself. Through sadhana and Divine Grace, we can experience our omniscient, omnipotent nature. When we succeed in that, we become Realized souls or *Jñanis*.

Amma says,

"Children, getting established in the attitude of witnessing is the real purpose of life. You may work and use your mind and your intellect; you may live in a house and have a family; you may have a lot of family responsibilities and you may have a lot of official duties to perform, but once you are established in that, in the real Center, you can do anything without moving out of that Center. Being in that state does not mean that you will remain idle without attending to your duties. You may be concerned about your children's studies, the health of your parents and your wife or husband and so on, yet in the midst of all these problems you remain a witness to all that happens and to all that you do. Within, you are perfectly still and unperturbed.

"While enacting the role of a villain in a movie, the actor may be shooting his enemy, getting angry, being cruel and treacherous, but within himself, does the actor really become angry or cruel? Is he really doing those things? Of course not; he is just a witness to all that he does. He mentally stands aside and acts without becoming involved or touched by it. He is not identified with the external expressions of his body. Likewise, one who is established in the state of witnessing remains untouched and unperturbed within under all circumstances."

Having the attitude of a witness is something that any one can practice. It is a question of persistent, conscious effort. Whenever we feel our usual calm giving way to anger, resentment, fear or desire, try to remain centered in your heart; stop and proceed with caution. Don't jump the gun. Practice detachment, non-reactiveness.

Thomas Jefferson said that, if you are angry, count to ten before saying anything. If you are very angry, count to one-hundred.

> "Do not walk around complaining that certain people got angry with you and that they criticized and scolded you. Let them even give a lecture criticizing you. Just keep quiet. Try to be calm. Your calmness will disarm the other person. When you react or retaliate, that means you have accepted what the other person has said about you, and then they will say even more things. There is no way to settle that kind of argument and the end-result is humiliation, anger, hatred, revenge, and the like. Why do you engage in such self-destructive processes? Observe silence, keep quiet. Or, if you want to accept it, receive it as God's gift. If you are very adamant and determined to accept it only as a demonic challenge, no one can save you from the final disaster, not even God."

—Amma

### Handling Criticism

Once there was a politician who did the best job he could. But being human, he made mistakes and was criticized. Reporters repeated his errors in the newspaper. He became so upset that he drove out into the country to visit his dear friend, a farmer. "What am I going to do?" the politician cried. "I've tried so hard. Nobody has tried harder than I have to do more good for more people, and look how they criticize me!"

But the old farmer could hardly hear the complaint of his persecuted politician friend because his hound dog was barking up a storm at the full moon. The farmer rebuked his dog, but the dog kept barking. Finally, the farmer said to the politician, "Do you want to know how you should handle your unfair critics? Here's how. Listen to that dog; now, look up at the moon and remember that, like the dog, people will keep yelling at you—they'll nip at your heels, and they'll criticize you. But here's the lesson: The dog keeps howling, but the moon keeps shining!"

This may seem impossible at first, but one success will lead to the next. What we must do is to be persistent and develop our will power through repeated effort. Amma lays a great deal of importance on self-effort. Ultimately, we will succeed in remaining a perfect witness even under the most trying circumstances. But however much we succeed, we must not lose our humility. Perhaps we should call this practice 'Devotional Witnessing." We should always keep in mind that our success in anything, our knowledge and understanding, are all due to our Guru's or God's grace. A truly great person is a humble person.

## Socrates' Humility

It is reported that the Oracle of Delphi declared Socrates as the wisest man on earth. So a few of his disciples went to him and said, "You should be happy. The Oracle has declared that you are the wisest man on earth."

Socrates laughed and said, "There must have been some mistake. How can I be the wisest man? I know only one thing, that I don't know anything. So there must have been some mistake. Go back and tell the Oracle."

They went back and told the Oracle, "Socrates has himself denied your statement, so there must be some mistake somewhere. He says that he is not wise, that he only knows that he knows nothing."

The Oracle said, "That is why I have declared that he is the wisest man, because only the wisest would say such a thing."

Only fools claim to be great. The beginning of real wisdom is to realize that you know nothing. Only then are you in a position to really learn something.

## A Young Artist

A young free-lance artist tried to sell his sketches to a number of newspapers. They all turned him down. One Kansas City editor told him he had no talent. But he had faith in his ability and kept trying to sell his work. Finally he got a job making drawings for church publicity material. He rented a mouse-infested garage to turn out his sketches and continued to produce free-lance drawings in the hope that someone would buy them.

One of the mice in the garage must have inspired him, for he created a cartoon character called Mickey Mouse. Walt Disney was on his way!

In order to develop that kind of will power and reach the state of being able to remain as a witness, other sadhanas are essential. Right now, most of us have dissipated and distracted minds. Because of this, our minds are weak. Take a thin thread and pull at it from both ends. It easily snaps. But if we twist a number of threads together into a cord, we can lift heavy objects with it. Similarly, when there are many diverse thoughts in the mind, each thought is weak. But if we can hold on to one single thought, the mind will become very strong and powerful, and we will experience increasing peace. This is the purpose of repeating a mantra. It will gradually reduce the many thoughts to one. From there it is easy to shut off all thought.

While doing this, in fact, while doing any practice that aims at quieting the mind, we may become tired and disappointed at the stubbornness of the mind. Sometimes just doing a lot of japa makes the mind dry. In fact, this is quite a common occurrence. Relax, take it easy for some time. There is no need to kill one's self to attain Realization. In fact, over-exertion can bring about a depressed mental state. It is like lifting too much weight with an undeveloped muscle.

## Anthony of the Desert

One day, the great monk, Anthony of the Desert, was relaxing with his disciples outside his hut when a hunter came by. The hunter was surprised to see Anthony relaxing and rebuffed him for taking it easy. It was not his idea of what a holy monk should be doing.

Anthony replied, "Bend your bow and shoot an arrow." The hunter did so. "Bend it again and shoot another arrow," said Anthony. The hunter did so, again and again.

The hunter finally said, "Brother Anthony, if I keep my bow always stretched, it will break."

"So it is with the monk," replied Anthony. "If we push ourselves beyond measure, we will break. It is right from time to time to relax our efforts."

When we are with Amma, let us forget about our worldly and even our spiritual problems. Sometimes our preoccupation with our problems blinds us to her Divine Presence. Let us bask in her blissful and healing presence that is radiating all around her. How many have commented on how much relief they feel both physically and mentally when near her. Take a dip in the Ocean of Bliss which is Amma and come out refreshed and ready to continue the journey back Home.

# CHAPTER TWELVE

# *Yearn for God*

"Remove the darkness of ignorance by thinking of God with a burning heart.

There should be total surrender to that One within in the form of one's own soul."

—Amma

We want to be happy, but many of us don't look for it where wise people say it is. Of course, all of us have found happiness in spirituality, at least to some degree. We know, through hearsay that we are the Supreme Light, but most us neither feel nor see it. We do not have the direct experience of Reality—*Aparokshanubhuti*. This can be a very frustrating stage in our journey back to God. There is a saying that there are only two carefree and happy people in this world: the completely ignorant and the completely wise. All the others struggle.

Because we don't have that bliss within, we continue to yearn to be happy. We yearn to be happy through whatever means are available, and then we feel sorrow because what we thought was going to make us happy doesn't, after some time. Such is the mystery we call life.

If we would yearn for the highest happiness, Amma says we would never be disappointed. But we should not stop until the goal is reached. We generally do not do so in relation to our worldly goals. We keep trying until we succeed. The *Upanishads* tell us: "Arise, awaken, stop not until the goal is reached!" This is very inspiring advice, and we should keep it in mind throughout our life. We must apply it to our spiritual life as well.

We will not be released from this sleepy darkness of ignorance until we give a very full-throated cry like a baby that really wants its mother. A mother calls her child to come home and have lunch, but the child is too busy playing to listen. The mother calls again and again to no avail. She finally gives up. After some time, the child feels real hunger and cries for the mother to take him home. This cry seems to be the precursor of God-realization, the intense cry to God or effort to reach Reality. We should be able to cry to God like Amma did.

> "O Mother, my heart is being torn by this pain of separation! Why does Your heart not melt seeing this endless stream of tears? O Mother, many Great Souls have adored You and thereby attained Your Vision and became eternally one with You. O Darling Mother! Please open the door of Your compassionate heart

for this humble servant of Yours! I am suffocating like one who is drowning. If You are not willing to come to me, then please put an end to my life.

"O Mother...here is Your child about to die drowning in unfathomable distress...this heart is breaking... these limbs are faltering...I am convulsing like a fish thrown on shore...O Mother...You have no kindness towards me...I have nothing left to offer You except the last breath of my life."

—Amma

Apparently, this kind of intensity of feeling and concentration is needed to break the illusion of Maya. Nothing belonging to creation can break Maya. It will be part of the dream. Only the absolute stillness of the mind centered on God can break the wheel or awaken us from our deep slumber. In that state, the truth that all is one will be experienced. That is the moment of liberation from all suffering and the attainment of bliss.

"There should be total surrender to that One within in the form of one's own soul."

—Amma

Don't consider God to be somewhere apart from you. That Being is your support, your source of energy and intelligence. We should try to learn what is meant by "surrender." It is summed up in Amma's words, "Don't worry, Amma is with you." In other words, lead your day-to-day life, acting in accordance with different situations as best as your intelligence can make out, accepting the results as God's will, and being at peace, in both pleasure and pain. As Lord Krishna says in the Bhagavad Gita:

"Verily this Divine Illusion of Mine, made up of the gunas or qualities of Nature, is hard to surmount. Whoever seeks Me alone, they cross over this Illusion."

—Ch. 7, v.14.

"Free from passion, fear and anger, absorbed in Me, taking refuge in Me, purified by the fire (tapas) of wisdom, many have reached My being."

—Ch.4,v.10

"That Goal should be sought for, whither having gone none return again. "I seek refuge in the Primeval Being whence streamed forth the Ancient Current."

—Ch.15, v.4

"The Lord dwells in the hearts of all beings, O Arjuna, whirling by Maya all beings (as if) mounted on a machine.

Fly unto Him for refuge with all thy being, O Bharata; by His Grace shall you obtain supreme peace (and) the eternal resting place."

—Ch. 18, v.61-62

# CHAPTER THIRTEEN

# Be Childlike, Not Childish

Devotee: Amma says that we should develop a child-like nature. But when I do this, I seem to get into a lot of trouble with others who disapprove of my immature actions and words. Am I doing something wrong?

Amma: We should become innocent like a child. Small children have certain qualities that adults should develop for making spiritual progress. But they also have some qualities that definitely should not be developed if one wants to be happy. This is due to their undeveloped intellectual faculty, which normally should mature with age. Adults grow up physically, but some continue to remain childish.

First, let us consider the qualities that should not be developed.

**Selfishness**: Most children are extremely selfish. They consider only what they want, and they will cry, throw tantrums and get very angry if they cannot get what they want. This is a childish quality that no adult should have, yet many adults do have this quality. This is because, as

Amma says, even though their bodies have grown up, their intellects have not matured.

**Lack of Discrimination**: They speak and do many meaningless things without thinking of the consequences. In other words, they do not have much of a sense of discrimination regarding what should and should not be said and done.

**Irresponsible**: They do not have a sense of responsibility and do what they feel like doing. They have no sense of duty or propriety.

"Children, a mother must have great patience in bringing up her children. A mother has to mold the child's character. The child learns his first lessons of love and patience from his mother. She cannot simply talk about love and patience and expect her son or daughter to adopt those qualities. No, that is impossible. She has to set an example of love and patience by putting those qualities into practice in all her dealings with her child.

"A child can be very adamant and uncompromising, of course, but that is the nature of most children since their minds are not fully developed. Caring only about their own needs, they can be very selfish and stubborn. But, that is permissible, for it is not contrary to the laws of nature. But if a mother becomes stubborn and impatient, that is very damaging.

That will create a hell. A mother must be patient, patient like the earth.

"A father is just as deeply involved in rearing the children as the mother. A father, too, must have patience. When a father grows impatient, that is the end of the child's innocent and trusting life. He or she will grow up to be impatient and adamant, never having experienced what it meant to be patient since nobody had demonstrated what it was. Socially, such a child has a difficult time. Friends will not be patient; girlfriends or boyfriends cannot be expected to have patience. Society is not going to be patient with an impatient boy or girl. Children will not have an opportunity to learn patience and love from anybody else if they do not learn these qualities from their parents.

"Children express what is taught to them and what they have experienced while growing up. Therefore, you should be very careful and cautious for your children's sake. Be careful about what you say. Be careful about what you do, because each word that you utter and each deed you perform creates a deep impression in your child's mind. It goes deep into his heart because those are the first things that he sees and hears. They are the first impressions indelibly imprinted upon his or her mind. The mother is the first person with whom the child is in contact.

Next comes the father. After that, the elder brothers and sisters. All other relationships come later in life. Therefore, in front of your children exercise control over your mind. Create a good home environment for them in which they can grow up. Otherwise, you will have many worries in the future."

The childlike qualities that Amma encourages us to develop are:

**Living in the present:** Children rarely think of the past or the future. They are absorbed in the present and so, if their circumstances are not painful, they are always carefree and happy. The burden of worry seems to be an adult quality.

**Equality towards all:** A child does not judge people. A man or woman, whatever the color, religion or nationality, whether rich or poor, young or old, is the same in a small child's eyes. Children generally trust anybody and are afraid of no one.

**No strong attachment towards anything:** A child may be playing with a toy that seems so dear to it, but the next moment it may leave it and go for a new toy. Even if something is taken away from it, the sorrow is extremely short-lived. Even its relationships with people may be similar, except in the case of its closest relatives like mother or father, sister or brother.

**No sexual attraction:** They have no sexual attractions

or sense of differentiation based on sex. All women are mommy, all men are daddy. They do not suffer from the distraction that grown people have. They live in their own blissful world of simplicity and innocence.

**Anger is short-lived:** Their anger lasts only for a short time. They will not hold a grudge against someone for long, unlike adults. They do not consider people evil, even if they are. It is said that King Yudhisthira, of Mahabharata fame, had no enemies and saw no evil people, even though thousands of people tried to kill him during the war. His cousin Duryodhana, saw only evil in people and could see no good in others.

**A sense of wonder and spontaneity:**

A little boy was in a village, away from the big city for the first time in his life. He was standing on the sidewalk when an old man drove up in a horse cart and went into a shop. The boy kept gazing in wonder at the horse, an animal he had never seen in his life. When the old man came out of the shop and was preparing to drive away, the kid said, "Hey, Mister! I ought to warn you that he just lost his petrol!"

Across the street in a fruit stall, there was a little girl with a banana peel in her hand: "What is it you want, darling?" said the vendor.

"A refill," was the reply.

# CHAPTER FOURTEEN

# Work Should Become Worship

M any devotees feel that they are unable to find the time to do much spiritual practice, either due to their busy life or lack of will power. Some also feel distracted by their work. They feel torn between two worlds, the spiritual, which they enjoy to some extent at home or in the ashram, and the work-a-day world. The contrast is too much for them. Amma says, "Children, make all of your actions into worship of God," but realistically speaking, is this even possible?

Some people achieve peace through a lot of meditation and a life of solitude. Others achieve it through the constant remembrance of God or Guru while doing all of their actions. Both are difficult. After all, bringing the restless mind under control is no easy task.

In order to have our work become worship, we need to develop a devotional state of mind at other times. When we first wake up in the morning, we should immediately meditate and pray for a few moments while sitting on the bed, instead of rushing to the bathroom or the kitchen or to read the newspaper. When we pray, we can ask God to accept all of the day's actions as His worship and request that our mind should flow towards Him like the Ganga flows toward the ocean. During the day, we can do *japa* while on the way to and from work. After coming home and finishing dinner and spending some time with the family, we should spend time reading the Bhagavad Gita and Srimad Bhagavatam. Otherwise, we can read the teachings of our Guru. If possible, we can sing some bhajans and recite some prayers. Before lying down to sleep, ask God for forgiveness for any mistakes we have made during the daytime and ask that our sleep should be one long prostration to Him.

Once a month, we can spend the whole day in sadhana, either in the house or, better yet, away from the house in a beautiful, secluded spot. I can speak for myself. When I used to live in Berkeley before leaving for India in 1968, I used to spend a lot of time up in the hills away from people—studying, meditating and praying. It helped me a lot.

> "Solitude is essential. We need to spend time doing only sadhana to purify our minds by getting rid of the bad vasanas we have accumulated in the past. Solitude will prevent the mind from being distracted and the mind will thus turn inward."
>
> —Amma

In this way, gradually, a current of God-remembrance and peace will begin to pervade our daily existence. We will become aware of the thoughts and actions that spoil our peace, and thus try to change our ways. We will start to feel peaceful even in stressful situations. Things will not upset us like they used to. We will become a lot less reactive and more of a witness, a spectator, rather than always reacting, going up and down with every pleasure and pain.

Those who choose solitude over life in the world will also have to deal with their negative vasanas. Mahatmas say the vasanas or habits are the main obstruction to our experiencing the peace which is hidden within us, behind the thinking mind. The problem is, most of them are invisible and unknown to us, residing as they do in the subconscious mind. Through prolonged and deep meditation, they will eventually come to the surface so that we become aware of them and take steps to destroy them. However, it would seem that the way of the yogi in the cave is a much slower and painful one than one who strives to remember God at all times and under all circumstances. The latter's vasanas will be exposed when circumstances arise that bring them up. Those who do intense sadhana while out in the world get their vasanas exhausted more quickly, gradually and in a natural way due to interaction with the world.

When we live in the world or with others, we have plenty of opportunities to uproot anger, one of the most common and powerful destructive habits. How will it be possible to know the extent of our latent anger while sitting alone in a cave?

At the very beginning of my spiritual life, I saw something that left a lifelong impression on me. I had just arrived at Arunachala, when an elderly devotee from the ashram there offered to take me for a tour of some of the holy spots in and around Tiruvannamalai. We saw many caves on the Holy Hill and some small temples as well. Then we went to a cave at a place called Pazhavakunram Hill, where a yogi had been staying for many years. We were standing some distance from the cave when a shepherd came there with a few goats. Suddenly, the yogi came running out of the cave in a rage and shouted at the shepherd, saying that he would kill all the goats if the shepherd didn't stop coming there and disturbing his meditation!

This demonstration of anger by a person who was sitting for years in a cave meditating really shocked me. It did not seem to be something I would like to do. It no doubt took a great deal of will power, but it did not seem to weaken the hidden darkness of the ego.

A devotee who desires the grace of God should always guard his or her speech. Speech is very powerful, not only for those who hear it, but equally, if not more so, for those who say it. It can purify the atmosphere or pollute it, and this goes for one's own mind.

### Diamonds and Toads

Once upon a time, there was a woman who had two daughters. The elder daughter was very much like her mother in face and manner. They were both so disagreeable and proud that there was no living with them.

The younger daughter was like her father, for she was good and sweet-tempered and very beautiful. As people naturally love their own likeness, the mother was very fond of her elder daughter, and at the same time had a great dislike for the younger. She made her eat on the floor in the kitchen and work all the time. Sort of reminds one of Cinderella.

Among other things, this poor child was obliged to go twice a day to draw a large pitcher of water from the spring in the woods two miles from the house.

One day, when she reached the spring, a poor woman came to her and begged for a drink.

"Oh yes! Certainly, ma'am," said the sweet little girl. She took some clear, cool water from the spring and held up the pitcher so that the woman might drink easily.

When she had finished, the woman said, "You are so very sweet, my dear, so good and so kind, that I cannot help giving you a gift."

Now this person was actually a fairy, who had taken the form of a poor country woman to see how this girl would treat her. "The gift I give you is," continued the fairy, "that with every word you speak, either a flower or a jewel shall come out of your mouth."

When the girl reached home, her mother scolded her for staying so long at the spring. "I beg your pardon Mamma," said the poor girl, "for not making more haste." And, as she spoke, there came out of her mouth two roses, two pearls, and two large diamonds.

"What is it I see here?" asked her mother, very surprised. "I think I see pearls and diamonds coming out of the girl's mouth! How did this happen, my child?" This was the first time she had ever called her "my child," or spoken kindly to her.

The poor child told her mother all that had happened at the spring and of the old woman's gift. All the time jewels and flowers fell from her lips.

"This is delightful," cried the mother. "I must send my other child to the spring. Come, girl, see what comes out of your sister's mouth when she speaks! Would you not be glad to have the same gift given to you? All you will have to do is to take the pitcher to the spring in the woods. When a poor woman asks you for a drink, give it to her."

"It would be a fine thing for me to do," said the selfish girl. "I will not go to draw water! My sister can give me her jewels. She does not need them."

"Yes, you will," said the mother, "and you will go this minute."

At last, the elder daughter went, grumbling and cursing all the way, taking with her the best silver pitcher in the house.

She had no sooner reached the spring then she saw a beautiful lady coming out of the wood. She came up and asked her for a drink. This was the same fairy who had met her younger sister, but now she had taken the form of a princess.

"I did not come out here to serve you with water," said the proud, selfish maid. "Do you think I brought this silver pitcher so far just to give you a drink? You can draw water from the spring as well as I."

"You are not very polite," said the fairy. "Since you are so rude and so unkind, the gift I give you is that, at every word you speak, toads and serpents shall come out of your mouth."

As soon as the mother saw her daughter coming, she cried out, "Well, my dear child, did you see the good fairy?"

"Yes, Mother," answered the proud girl, and as she spoke, two serpents and two toads fell from her mouth.

"What is this that I see?" cried the mother. "What have you done?"

The girl tried to answer but, at every word, toads and serpents came from her lips.

And so it was forever after. Jewels and flowers fell from the lips of the younger daughter, who was so good and kind, while the elder daughter could not speak without a shower of serpents and toads.

When we have succeeded in awakening the inner current of God-remembrance, a unique stillness will be felt behind all our thoughts and emotions. Even during activities, we will be able to hold on to that with 'one hand' while the 'other hand' engages in work. Gradually, we will feel detached from all our actions and rest in that peace, even if we are working intensely. In fact, meditation while working is an extremely effective sadhana. We become like an actor on the stage, playing our part but not identifying with it. Then we will understand the meaning of Shakespeare's words:

> All the world's a stage,
> And all the men and women merely players;
> They have their exits and their entrances,
> And one man in his time plays many parts,
> His acts being seven ages...

### Fighting Without Anger

A story worth telling happened in the life of a king, who had succeeded in dedicating even his fighting to God. He was fighting with a very strong enemy for thirty years. In the end, it happened one day that an opportunity came. The enemy fell off his horse and the king jumped on him with his spear. In just one second, the spear would have pierced the heart of the man, and everything would have been finished. But in that small gap, the enemy did one thing: he spat on the king's face and the spear stopped. The king touched his face, got up and told the enemy, "Tomorrow we start again."

The enemy was puzzled. He said: "What is the matter? We have been waiting for this for thirty years. I have been hoping that someday or other I would be on your chest with my spear and the thing would be finished. That opportunity never came to me, but it has now come you. You could have finished me off in a single moment. What is the matter with you?"

The king said: "This has not been an ordinary war. I have taken a vow that I will fight without anger. For thirty years, I was fighting without anger. But, just for a moment, anger now came. When you spat, I felt angry and it became personal. I wanted to kill you; the ego came up. Up to now, for thirty years that was not a problem at all, we were fighting for a cause. You were not my enemy, it was not personal in any way; I was not in any way interested in killing you. I just wanted the cause to win. But, for a moment, I forgot about the cause. You were my enemy and I wanted to kill you. That is why I cannot kill you. So, tomorrow we start again."

But the war never started again because the enemy became a friend. He said: "Now teach me. Be my master and let me be your disciple. I would also like to fight without anger."

The Bhagavad Gita teaches this principle of detached action in a crystal clear manner:

"Treating alike pleasure and pain, gain and loss, success and defeat, prepare for the battle (of life)."

—Ch. 2, v. 38

"Therefore, without attachment, constantly perform the action that should be done. Performing action without attachment, man reaches the Supreme."

—Ch. 3, v.19

"Renouncing all action in Me, with thy thought resting on the Self, being free from hope, free from selfishness, devoid of feverishness, do thou fight. Those who constantly practice this teaching with faith and without complaining, they too are liberated from actions."

— Ch. 3, v. 30-31

"By the body, by the mind, by the intellect, by mere senses also, yogis perform action, without attachment, for the purification of the self. The steady-minded one, abandoning the fruit of action, attains the peace born of devotion. The unsteady one, attached to the fruit through the action of desire, is firmly bound."

—Bhagavad Gita, Ch. 5, 11-12

By studying a Master's teachings or associating with a great being such as Amma, we gain the faith that the teachings of spirituality are the ultimate truth. The true nature of the individual being, much subtler than the body and mind, is the subtlest principle of indestructible consciousness, the *Atman* or 'I'. The Atman and its source, Brahman, the Supreme Reality, are one in essence, like a spark and fire. Spirituality is the way of life oriented to the ultimate purpose or goal of life, which is the realization or direct experience of the oneness of Atman with the Supreme Being or God. Until this is experienced, the individual continues to take birth in body after body in the beginningless cycle of birth, death and rebirth called *samsara*. The techniques of transcending identification with the body-mind complex are called Yoga, which must be practiced until the attainment of Liberation from samsara.

**Guard Your Faith**

"If you lose your faith, a sorrowful sense of futility will proliferate."

—Amma

How do we lose this faith? Sometimes, due to associating with people or books that encourage pure materialism, faith is shaken. We lose our spiritual direction or purpose and feel that only materialism makes sense. Even the place in which we live and the food we eat may bring about such a change. If we go the way of materialism, we will eventually become disillusioned, perhaps in this life or a future one, for the iindividual soul or *jiva* can never be satisfied with materialism. Why not? Because we are, in essence, spirit temporarily bound to a body. In this vast Creation, we are constantly wandering in search of lasting happiness. We can reach the state of fulfillment only by merging into our spiritual source. This is why Amma says that, if you lose your way, a sorrowful sense of futility will overtake you.

"Give attention to the essence of Amma's advice and cultivate internal purity. Then children, the Divine World of Eternal Bliss will shine forth within you."

—Amma

What is the essence of Amma's teaching? Realize the Self. How to go about it? The first step is the cultivation of internal purity. Purity of the body, bathing it and keeping it clean, will not bring about internal purity. If it would, ducks and fish would have pure minds and would all be saints. Inner purity means purity of the mind. We all know what pure and impure thoughts are. Pure thoughts make us feel peaceful and happy. Impure thoughts agitate us and make us restless and unhappy. We must discriminate between the two, rejecting the former and cultivating the later. This is not an easy task. Out of ignorance of real spirituality, we have been indulging in impure, worldly thoughts for ages. All spiritual practice is for purifying the mind of the rajasic and tamasic thoughts and increasing the sattvic ones. All sadhana is for that. Eventually, even the sattvic thoughts must be rejected for the Divine Nature to dawn.

The Divine World of Eternal Bliss is within us; it is the very nature of the purified mind. "The Kingdom of Heaven is within you," said Christ. Whatever of the many worlds we may live in, our inner feeling will be one of joy, of unchanging, undiluted bliss and peace. When the mind is restless, that is itself hell. Even if one is actually in hell, a pure mind will be in bliss. That state is beyond pain.

### A Sufi Saint

Mansur Al-Hallaj was a famous Sufi of the 10th century. He was tortured and executed in 922 AD for having said "Ana al Haq," which means, "I am the Truth." He died with a smile on his face in the knowledge of the Self.

The Bhagavad Gita speaks of this state:

> When, having obtained It, he thinks no other acquisition superior to it; when, therein established, he is not moved even by great pain;

> This severance from union with pain, be it known, is called union (Yoga). That Yoga must be practiced with determination and with undepressed heart.

> Abandoning without reserve all fancy-born desires, well-restraining all the senses from all quarters by the mind;

> Little by little let him withdraw, by reason (buddhi) held in firmness; keeping the mind established in the Self, let him not think of anything.

> By whatever cause the wavering and unsteady mind wanders away, from that let him restrain it and bring it back direct under the control of the Self.

> Supreme Bliss verily comes to this Yogin, whose mind is quite tranquil, whose passion is quieted, who has become Brahman, who is blemishless.

> Thus, always keeping the self steadfast, the yogin, freed from sins, attains with ease to the infinite bliss of contact with the (Supreme) Brahman.

—Ch.6, v.22-28

# CHAPTER FIFTEEN

# *The Great Power of Maya*

"Maya, the Great Power of Illusion, is pushing us back from progressing spiritually. We are spending our days in body-consciousness with a heart full of sorrow. What a pity that the devil of desire, which affects us through illusory temptations, kicks us into the dark abyss of Maya making us the food for the god of Death. If you get caught in his grip, woe unto you, for you will lose your soul. All worries will come to an end if only you give up your desires and keep your hopes in God alone."

—Amma

Maya, the Divine Power of Illusion, is always pulling us down, away from God-realization, away from our source, the Ocean of Bliss. It makes us forget our Real Self and makes us identify with the perishable part of our self, the body and personality. Once that has happened, we will not know what real happiness is. Then we endlessly seek it through pleasure of the senses and the mind. We will always be experiencing alternating sorrow and happiness endlessly till death.

The only relief we seem to get is in dreamless sleep. Even death won't be the solution to this eternal problem. The same delusion will persist in the next world and even after that. Understanding this, and knowing that the only solution is Liberation, we should strive intensely for attaining that.

Sadly, Maya makes many things look attractive, as possible sources of pleasure and happiness, and blinds us to the ugly side of things, the painful possibilities or probabilities. Most of all, we are deluded by physical appearances. Physical beauty attracts everyone, yet we have all heard the expression: "All that glitters is not gold." A person may be well dressed, handsome or beautiful, but be a devil inside, and if we could look beneath the exterior, we would not feel so enchanted! Unfortunately, even after a lifetime of running after Maya, we still do not attain the happiness or lasting peace we desire. We keep doing the same things again and again, like a cow chewing the cud. And, unlike Amma, we cannot see the Imperishable in the perishable due to our gross vision.

The strangest thing is that, even when we hear, understand and know this to be true, we are unable to get serious about doing something about it to fix it. Even if we start to make our way back to the Truth, our ancient habits pull us back again and again into the ocean of samsara.

We feel that spiritual truths are just a wishful goal, not the urgent truth. We are like creatures on the bottom of the ocean, not at all inclined to swim to the surface and enjoy the light. Only when the tremendous seriousness of our situation dawns on us will we make the requisite effort to escape. Until then, Amma will be saying, "Do like this, my children," and we will be saying, "Not yet Amma. I still have other important things to do."

## The Rich Merchant

Once there was a very rich merchant, who owned many shops and warehouses. Between his office and house was a small Siva temple. On his way back home every night, he used to stop there and worship the Lord, unloading all his worries at His feet. He would pray, "O, Lord Siva, I am tired of this life. What worries, what work, what sleepless nights! Please relieve me of all these problems by taking me to Thy Feet!" This would be his prayer every day. But he would come to the temple very late after work, and this worried the priest of the temple. The temple was to be closed at 9 p.m., but the merchant would show up only after 10. This meant that the priest must stay up until the merchant was gone. He could not refuse to do so, either, for fear of losing his job, since the man was an influential person. He therefore prayed to the Lord for a way to stop this botheration.

Finally, the priest came up with a plan. It was 10 o'clock when the man arrived at the temple as usual. The priest hid behind the image of Lord Siva. The merchant began his usual prayer. "O Lord! I am tired of this miserable life. Please take me to Thy Feet." Hardly had he said this, when a booming voice came from the inner shrine. "Come, come to Me this minute and I will take you forever!" The man almost fainted from shock. After finding his voice, he cried out, "Lord! Pardon me, but I have a hundred duties to fulfill. My daughter's marriage is fixed for next week; my son has to be put into the medical college and my wife has not yet returned from my son-in-law's house. I have purchased another warehouse and the registration is this Friday. When I have settled all of these, I will come, O Lord!" Saying this, the merchant ran out of the temple and never again did the priest have to stay up late, for the man never returned!

Every day, we hear of successful and ambitious young people suddenly dying. *'Of course, that won't happen to me,'* we think. We keep succumbing to the fascination of Maya till the end. We get caught up in pursuing some goal or other, forgetting the truth, and become the "food for the god of Death." Only if we lead a life of dedication to the goal of spiritual realization will we go to God at the time of our departure from this world instead of to the *other* god (of death).

### Controlling Desires

The famous Russian author and philosopher, Leo Tolstoy, wrote a story that is a metaphor for the need for us to set boundaries on our desires, the great enticements of Maya. It nicely conveys the truth that, forgetting death, we may overdo the pursuit of our goals and finally become that god's breakfast.

There once was a peasant named Pahom, who worked hard and honestly for his family but had no land of his own, so he always remained poor. Close to Pahom's village there lived a lady, a small landowner, who had an estate of about three hundred acres. One winter, the news got about that the lady was going to sell her land. Pahom heard that a neighbor of his was buying fifty acres and that the lady had consented to accept one half in cash and to wait a year for the other half.

Pahom and his wife put their heads together and considered how they could manage to buy it. They had one hundred rubles laid by. They sold a colt, and one half of their bees, hired out one of their sons as a laborer, and took his wages in advance. They borrowed the rest from a brother-in-law, and so scraped together half the purchase money. Having done this, Pahom chose a farm of forty acres, some of it wooded, and went to the lady and bought it.

So now Pahom had land of his own. He borrowed seed and sowed it, and the harvest was a good one. Within a year, he had managed to pay off his debts to the lady and his brother-in-law. So he became a landowner, plowing and sowing his own land, making hay on his own land, cutting his own trees, and feeding his cattle on his own pasture.

Then, one day, Pahom was sitting at home when a peasant, passing through the village, happened to stop in. Pahom asked him where he came from, and the stranger answered that he came from beyond the Volga River where he had been working. One word led to another and the man went on to say that much land was for sale there, and that many people were moving there to buy it. The land was so good, he said, that one peasant had brought nothing with him but his bare hands, and now he had six horses and two cows of his own.

Pahom's heart was filled with desire. 'Why should I suffer in this narrow hole,' he thought, 'if one can live so well elsewhere? I will sell my land and my homestead here and, with the money, I will start fresh over there and get everything new.'

So Pahom sold his land and homestead and cattle, all at a profit, and moved his family to the new settlement. Everything the peasant had told him was true, and Pahom was ten times better off than he had been. He bought plenty of arable land and pasture, and could keep as many head of cattle as he liked.

At first, in the bustle of building and settling down, Pahom was pleased with it all, but when he got used to it, he began to think that, even here, he was not satisfied.

Then, one day, a passing land dealer said he was just returning from the land of the Bashkirs, far away, where he had bought thirteen thousand acres of land, all for only one thousand rubles.

"All one needs do is to make friends with the chiefs," he said. "I gave away about one hundred rubles' worth of dressing gowns and carpets, besides a case of tea, and I gave wine to those who would drink it, and I got the land for less than two pence an acre."

Pahom thought, 'Out there I can get more than ten times as much land as I have now. I must try it.'

So he left his family to look after the homestead and started on the journey, taking his servant with him. They stopped at a town on their way, and bought a case of tea, some wine, and other presents, as the tradesman had advised him. On and on they went until they had gone more than three hundred miles and, on the seventh day, they came to a place where the Bashkirs had pitched their tents.

As soon as they saw Pahom, they came out of their tents and gathered around their visitor. They gave him tea and plenty of food. Pahom took presents out of his cart and distributed them, and told them he had come about some land. The Bashkirs seemed very glad and told him he must talk to their chief about it. So they sent for him and explained to him why Pahom had come.

The chief listened for a while, then made a sign with his head for them to be silent, and, addressing himself to Pahom, said:

"Well, let it be so. Choose whatever piece of land you like. We have plenty of it."

"And what will be the price?" asked Pahom.

"Our price is always the same: one thousand rubles a day." Pahom did not understand.

"A day? What measure is that? How many acres would that be?"

"We sell it by the day. As much as you can go round on your feet in a day is yours, and the price is one thousand rubles."

Pahom was surprised. "But in a day you can get round a large tract of land," he said. The chief laughed.

"It will all be yours!" said he. "But there is one condition: if you don't return on the same day to the spot whence you started, your money is lost."

Pahom was delighted, but could not sleep that night. He kept thinking about the land.

'What a large tract I will mark off!' thought he. 'I can easily do thirty-five miles in a day. The days are long now, and within a circuit of thirty-five miles what a lot of land there will be!'

In the morning, the Bashkirs got ready and they all started. They ascended a hillock and, dismounting from their carts and their horses, gathered in one spot. The chief came up to Pahom and stretched out his arm toward the plain.

"See," said he, "all this, as far as your eye can reach, is ours. You may have any part of it you like."

Pahom's eyes glistened: it was all virgin soil, as flat as the palm of your hand, as black as the seed of a poppy, and, in the hollows, different kinds of grasses grew chest high. He took off his outer coat, put a little bag of bread into the pocket of his vest and, tying a flask of water to his pants, stood ready to start. He considered for some moments which way he had better go—it was tempting everywhere.

Pahom started walking neither slowly nor quickly. After having gone a thousand yards, he stopped, and concluded that he had walked three miles. It had grown quite warm now; he looked at the sun; it was time to think of breakfast.

'I will go on for another three miles,' he thought, 'and then turn to the left. This spot is so fine that it would be a pity to lose it. The further one goes, the better the land seems.'

He went straight on for a while, and when he looked round, the hillock was scarcely visible and the people on it looked like black ants, and he could just see something glistening there in the sun. 'Ah,' thought Pahom, 'I have gone far enough in this direction; it is time to return. Besides, I am very thirsty.'

He went on and on; the grass was high, and it was very hot. Pahom began to grow tired; he looked at the sun and saw that it was noon. 'Well,' he thought, 'I must have a rest.' He sat down and ate some bread and drank some water but thought, 'an hour to suffer, a lifetime to live,' so he started again.

He went a long way and then looked toward the hillock. The heat made the air hazy; it seemed to be quivering, and, through the haze, the people on the hillock could scarcely be seen. He looked at the sun: it was nearly halfway to the horizon, and he was still ten miles from the goal.

Pahom went straight toward the hillock, but he now walked with difficulty. He was exhausted from the heat, his bare feet were cut and bruised, and his legs began to fail. He longed to rest, but that was impossible if he meant to get back before sunset. The sun waits for no man, and it was sinking lower and lower.

Pahom walked on and on; it was very hard walking, but he went quicker and quicker. He pressed on, but was still far from the place. He began running. 'What shall I do,' he thought again. 'I have grasped too much, and ruined the whole affair. I can't get there before the sun sets.'

And this fear made him still more breathless. Pahom went on running, his soaking shirt and trousers stuck to him, and his mouth was parched. His chest was working like a blacksmith's bellows, his heart was beating like a hammer, and his legs were giving way as if they did not belong to him.

Pahom was seized with terror lest he should die of the strain. Though afraid of death, he could not stop. 'After having run all that way, they will call me a fool if I stop now.' So he ran on and on, and drew near and heard the Bashkirs yelling and shouting to him, and their cries inflamed his heart still more. He gathered his last strength and ran on.

The sun was close to the horizon and was about to set! The sun was quite low, but he was also quite near his aim. Pahom could already see the people on the hillock waving their arms to hurry him up. With all his remaining strength he rushed on, bending his body forward so that his legs could hardly follow fast enough to keep him from falling. Just as he reached the hillock, it suddenly grew dark. He looked up—the sun had already set! He gave a cry: "All my labor has been in vain!" He was about to stop, when he heard the Bashkirs still shouting, and remembered that, though to his view from below, the sun seemed to have set, they on the hillock could still see it. He took a long breath and ran up the hillock. It was still light there. He reached the top. There sat the chief, laughing and holding his sides. Pahom uttered a cry; his legs gave way beneath him and he fell forward. Pahom was dead!

His servant picked up the spade and dug a grave long enough for Pahom to lie in, and buried him in it. Six feet from his head to his heels was all he needed!

# CHAPTER SIXTEEN

# God is the Doer

## Only the Grace of God Can Remove Vasanas

In one of the battles between the celestials and the demons, the former won a victory over the latter. Such battles are going on at all times in all levels of Consciousness, between the positive and negative forces of virtue and vice. Sometimes, the positive forces win and at other times the negative forces have the victory. In this particular instance, the celestials were victorious; they became proud and thought that the victory was due to their strength, forgetting the Unseen Power behind all actions, described as the Life of life, or the Lord, the Divine Power.

In order to remove this vanity—a stumbling block in the spiritual path—the compassionate Supreme Brahman, the Omniscient, Pure Consciousness, appeared before them in the form of a mysterious spirit, a *yaksha*, a super-human, incredibly mighty, gigantic form that the celestials had never seen before. They were taken aback by the appearance of this most wonderful Being.

Agni, the god of fire, was deputed to find out who or what exactly that Being was. Before the fire god could start his inquiry, he was, on the other hand, himself subjected to an inquiry by that yaksha. On being asked as to who he was and what power he had, the fire god vainly replied that he was the well-known fire god, the foremost among celestials and capable of burning the whole world down, thus himself giving an occasion for his power to be tested. That Being placed a piece of dry straw in front of Agni and asked him to burn it. He could not burn it, for the yaksha, the Supreme Power behind all actions, had withdrawn that power of burning from him. Agni could not even touch it or shake it, a little piece of dry straw! With his head bent down out of shame and frustration, Agni returned to the gods.

Then it was the turn of Vayu, the wind god, to go and inquire about the real nature of the yaksha. When asked the same thing that had been asked to Agni, he also met with the same fate. "I can blow away everything on earth!" replied Vayu proudly. The yaksha put a blade of grass in front of him and asked him to blow it away. Vayu tried, but it did not move at all. He tried again with all his might, but the blade of grass did not move even slightly. His ego was crushed. Embarrassed and crestfallen, he did not even remember to ask the yaksha who he was, and returned humiliated.

Next, Indra, the king of the celestials, the emperor of the three worlds himself went, thinking that what other gods could not do, perhaps he could achieve himself being their king. Indra was certainly more powerful than the other gods under him.

Indra prepared to go, but when he reached the spot, the yaksha disappeared. In his place, he saw a beautiful woman. It was the Goddess Parvati. Indra asked her about the yaksha, and she said, "The yaksha was the Divine Being Himself. It is due to His Power that you were victorious against the demons." Hearing this, Indra realized that the gods had been unwittingly conceited and that the power behind everything and everyone is that of the Supreme Being, the invisible All-doer. He humbly departed and Parvati disappeared. Indra then informed the gods. Being the first gods to attain the knowledge of the all-doership of the Supreme Spirit, he was considered to be the greatest amongst them.

One lesson to be learned from this story is that negative vasanas can be overcome only by the grace of God. Without His strength and Will, even a blade of grass cannot move. Humility is a prerequisite for learning spiritual principles. We should constantly remember that He is running the show and is taking care of even the least of us. True humility comes about through the awareness of

His Presence within our mind. A mere devotional attitude is not enough for that to happen. It must become a direct experience born out of intense sadhana and surrender.

In the words of that great soul of renunciation and faith, Christ said:

> "Consider the lilies of the field, how they grow; they neither toil nor spin; yet I tell you, even Solomon in all his glory was not arrayed like one of these. But if God so clothes the grass of the field, which today is alive and tomorrow is thrown into the oven, will He not much more clothe you, O you of little faith? Therefore do not be anxious, saying, 'What shall we eat?' or 'What shall we drink?' or 'What shall we wear?' Seek first His kingdom and His righteousness, and all these things shall be yours as well.

Behind every incident in this world, whether big or small, significant or insignificant, He alone is, and it is His power that does everything. He alone is the cause of the victory of the winner as well as the defeat of the vanquished. He works miracles and every incident in our life, if only we go deep into its cause, will be seen to be a miracle. He is everywhere and still He cannot be seen as we see an object or person. Thus should one meditate on Him, as the Ultimate Cause of all that happens here in this world and all the other worlds.

"Surrender comes through the realization of your own helplessness. The realization that all that you claim as yours—your intellect, beauty and charm, your health and wealth—are nothing before the great and imminent threat of death. Death will snatch everything away. This realization wakes you up. You become alert. You realize that you are laying claim on things that are not really yours. Therefore, surrender. You can enjoy life's many pleasures, but you should do so with the awareness that it may be taken away at any time. If you live life with this awareness, surrender will follow.

Until you realize that you are helpless, that your ego cannot save you, and that all you have acquired is nothing, God or Guru will keep on creating circumstances necessary to make you realize this truth. When that happens, you will surrender. That is when you cast off all your fear and let the Guru or God dance on your ego while you lay low at His Feet. That is when you become a true devotee. This is the real meaning of prostration.

"The final destiny for all souls is the dropping away of every obstruction to peace and contentment. When that moment comes, the ego is dropped, and you won't struggle anymore. You will neither protest, nor will you even pause to think whether you should let go or not. You will just bow down and surrender. Deep within, every soul is waiting for this great letting go to happen.

"A real prayer will never contain any suggestions, instructions or demands. The sincere devotee will simply say 'O Lord, I do not know what is good or what is bad for me. I am nobody—nothing. You know everything. I know whatever You do must be for the best; therefore, do as You wish.' In real prayer, you bow down, surrender and declare your helplessness to the Lord."

—Amma

The difference between a spiritually minded person and one who is not, is in their attitude towards life, not in their experiences. Everyone gets his or her share of pleasure and pain. Two people may have similar experiences, but may react to them differently. One benefits and grows in wisdom, while the other does not. A devotee sees the Hand of God in everything that happens. However, only a mahatma can truly understand His intentions or Will.

**Be Yourself**

Once upon a time in Japan, there was a poor stone-cutter named Hofus. He used to go everyday to the mountainside to cut great blocks of stone. He lived near the mountain in a little stone hut and worked hard and was happy.

One day, he took a load of stone to the house of a rich man. There he saw so many beautiful things. When he went back to his mountain, he could think of nothing else. Then he began to wish that he, too might sleep in a bed as soft as down, with curtains of silk and tassels of gold. And he sighed, "Ah me! Ah me! If only Hofus were rich as he!"

To his surprise, the voice of the Mountain Spirit answered, "Have thou thy wish!"

When Hofus returned home that evening, his little hut was gone, and in its place stood a great palace. It was filled with beautiful things, and the best of all was a bed of down, with curtains of silk and tassels of gold.

Hofus decided to work no more, but he was not used to being idle, and time passed slowly; the days seemed very long.

One day, as he sat by the window, he saw a carriage dash past. It was drawn by snow-white horses. In it sat a prince, while before and behind were servants in suits of blue and white. One was holding a golden umbrella over the prince. When the stone-cutter saw this, he began to feel unhappy, and he sighed, "Ah me! Ah me! If only Hofus a prince might be!"

And again the same voice that he had heard on the mountain answered, "Be thou a prince!"

Straightway, Hofus became a prince. He had servants dressed in crimson and gold, and he rode in a carriage with a golden umbrella over his head.

For a short time he was happy, but, one day, as he walked in the garden, he saw that the flowers were drooping and the grass was dry and brown, and when he rode out, he felt the hot sun burn him in spite of his umbrella.

"The sun is mightier than I," he thought, and then he sighed. "Ah me! Ah me! If Hofus only the sun might be!"

And the voice answered, "Be thou the sun!"

Straightway he became the great sun. He burned the grass and rice fields. He dried up the streams. Rich and poor alike suffered from the terrible heat.

One day, a cloud came and rested in front of him, and hid the earth from his sight. He was angry and cried, "Ah me! Ah me! If Hofus only a cloud might be!"

And the voice answered, "Be thou a cloud!" Straightway, a cloud he became. He floated before the face of the sun, and hid the earth from it.

Then, day after day, the cloud dropped rain. The rivers overflowed and the rice-fields were covered with water. Towns were swept away. Only the great rocks on the mountainside stood unmoved midst the flood. The cloud looked at them in wonder, then he sighed. "Ah me! Ah me! If Hofus only a rock might be!"

And the voice answered, "Be thou a rock!"

Straightway, a rock he became. Proudly he stood. The sun could not burn him and the rain could not move him.

"Now, at last," he said, "no one is mightier than I."

But one day he was awakened from his dreams by a noise, tap! tap! tap! down at his feet. He looked and there was a stone-cutter driving his tool into the rock. Another blow and the great rock shivered; a block of stone broke away. "That man is mightier than I!" cried Hofus, and he sighed. "Ah me! Ah me! If Hofus only the man might be!"

And the voice answered, "Be thou thyself!" And straightway Hofus was himself again, a poor stone-cutter, working all day upon the mountainside, going home at night to his little hut. But now he was content and happy, and never again did he wish to be other than Hofus the stone-cutter.

A man lay down on his bed and dreamed that he traveled all over the universe. At last, he woke up and found himself in his own bed. Such is the dream of Maya in which we are all immersed!

# CHAPTER SEVENTEEN

# *Wake Up, Wake Up!*

"Children, make your mind pure and then understand the essence of dharma. If you perpetuate the evil desire for ever-new things, it will lead to disappointment."

—Amma

Devotee: Why do people make mistakes?

Amma: "We are caught in the illusion that we will get happiness from the world. Then we madly run here and there to acquire it. Having unfulfilled desires, frustration and anger result. Without discriminating between the necessary and the unnecessary, we do anything we like. Can we say that this is life? Whose fault is it?"

Devotee: It is said that without God's presence and will, even a blade of grass cannot bend in a breeze. Can human beings then be blamed for errors if God is making them do everything?

Amma: "For a person who has the conviction, "The real doer is not me, but God," it is impossible to commit any mistakes. He sees everything permeated by God. It is impossible for that devotee to even think about making mistakes. To say it in another way, only someone who has transcended all errors will have the faith, "God alone is the doer, even a blade of grass will not move without Him." There is no error or sin for one who has the conviction that God is the doer, whereas the fruits of the mistakes committed by a person who feels, "I am the doer" must be accepted by him. Having committed a murder, it is not right to say that God is the doer. One whose thought is, "God is the doer" would not commit murder, would he?"

### The Brahmin Who Killed a Cow

There was once an old brahmin who owned a beautiful garden. He loved the garden dearly and spent a lot of time tending to it. One day, when the brahmin came out to see how his mango saplings were doing, he found, to his utter dismay, that a stray cow had wandered into his garden and was eating the saplings he had planted with so much care. In a fit of rage, he began to beat the cow with his stick. The thin old cow couldn't take the beating and dropped dead on the spot.

"O God! What have I done! I have killed a cow," the brahmin lamented. The news reached the villagers and they came to the brahmin's house. "You have committed the greatest of sins by killing a cow," one of them scolded. "You have put your garden above the life of the cow." Another villager added, "The cow gives us milk. She is our mother, and you killed her!" "What kind of hand is yours that can kill a cow?" the village leader asked. "You will have to suffer the consequences for what you have done. We are leaving now, but we will be back."

'They will throw me out of the village. What shall I do?' thought the brahmin.

Suddenly, he had an idea. 'Lord Indra is the god that presides over the hands,' he thought to himself. 'So it is Indra, not me, that should be blamed for killing the cow. Yes, I will tell the villagers that!'

The villagers were not sure what to make of the brahmin's argument. It was indeed true that Lord Indra is the presiding deity over the hands. Did that mean that the brahmin should not be blamed for killing the cow? The question was debated far and wide.

Ultimately, Indra himself heard of the brahmin's argument. He was troubled by the brahmin's logic and decided to pay him a visit. Taking the form of an old man, Indra casually came into the brahmin's garden.

"Sir, I am a stranger to this town," Indra said to the brahmin. "I was just passing this way and I noticed this beautiful garden. Did you make it all by yourself?"

The brahmin was greatly flattered. "Yes indeed, with my own hands. I have tended to this garden like it is my own child."

"I can see that!" Indra replied. "And how about this beautiful path? Did you also lay it down?"

"Certainly!" the brahmin replied with great pride. "I laid it myself with lots of planning."

"And this beautiful tree?" Indra continued. "Did you also plant it yourself?"

"Of course!" the brahmin proclaimed. "From the ploughing to the fruit, it is all my work!"

"Wow! And how about the fountain?" questioned Indra.

"Everything you see here was set up by me with my own hands," the brahmin boasted.

At this, Indra revealed himself to the brahmin and said, "O brahmin, if you take the credit for setting up your garden with your own hands, then shouldn't you take the blame for killing the cow too? Why blame me for that, you rascal?"

From one viewpoint, everything is His will. From another viewpoint, we have our duties. The company may run according to the basic principles laid down by the CEO or owner, but the individual employees have their own responsibilities. The CEO cannot be responsible for the mischief or mistakes of the employees since he has already laid down the rules.

The Lord creates the universe with its laws of dharma and adharma. We reap the fruits accordingly. He is the *karma phala data*, the Giver of the fruits of the actions done by us. In that sense, everything is His will, but this does not exempt us from responsibility.

> "If we are the doers of deeds, we should reap the fruits they yield. But when we question, 'Who am I, the doer of this deed?' and realize the Self, the sense of agency is lost and the three karmas slip away. Eternal is this Liberation."
>
> —Ramana Maharshi, Reality in Forty Verses, v.38

Once we gain purity of mind through spiritual practice, it becomes clearer as to what is right action. We may still make mistakes—no one is perfect, but we will be able to more clearly intuit the way of dharma in our thoughts, words and actions. Generally, we cannot trust our feelings and should follow scripture, tradition, or the way shown by elders. This is the accepted way of learning what dharma is. Eventually, by doing so for a long time, purity dawns; then our actions become more spontaneously dharmic.

### Madness of Consumerism

More than any time in the past, consumerism has become all-pervasive, even in so-called remote regions. People have become crazy for material possessions, far beyond their daily needs. Unfortunately, it doesn't stop there. Upgrades of everything keep coming endlessly. I heard of someone who buys every new laptop that comes on the market. I wonder what he does with all of the 'old' ones. It seems like humanity is hypnotized into going to the 'fulfillment centers' to get fulfilled. Of course, they never do get fulfilled. How can possessions fulfill one? If we continuously run after things without discriminating between what is really necessary and what is not, we will eventually become very disappointed.

Amma warns that the desire for newer and newer things will lead to disappointment, and that this is not a habit that one should encourage in oneself or others.

In every field of work or entertainment, there are always newer and newer things coming into existence. In every field of life, we are becoming enamored of the newer and newer. Where is it all leading? Ultimately and hopefully, to God, the Ever-new One. But this will happen not from a sense of fulfillment, but rather through a sense of disillusionment and disappointment. Only then will we look within for the happiness of our Self.

**Hiding the Nectar**

Once, after retrieving the Nectar of Immortality from the churning of the cosmic ocean, the gods decided to hide it so human beings could not find it. They thought very deeply about it since they wanted to hide it somewhere where it could never be found. Some suggested to Indra, the king of the gods, that they should hide it in the highest peaks of the Himalayas, but he said no, since many humans would climb it one day.

Someone else said, "Let us hide it in the deepest part of the ocean, since no human can retrieve it from there."

Indra said, "No, one day humans will be able to move under the oceans riding inside a vehicle."

Another god suggested that they hide it on the moon saying, "No humans will ever be able to reach there." But Indra did not agree, and seeing into the future he said, "No, humans will one day also travel to the Moon, and they will certainly find it there."

Not able to come to any conclusion, they approached Brahma, the Creator. After saluting him, they presented their problem to him and asked for his advice.

Brahma thought about it for a while and finally said, "I have thought of a place where humans will never look. You should place the nectar within the human heart, for no one will ever look for it there."

Brahma was so right. Even though this nectar is so close to human beings, it is also so far, for no one ever bothers to look for it within themselves.

This is not to say that worldly life has no value, but every lifetime is spent in pursuit of worldly goals and still there is no peace or contentment. Why do people continue to think that worldly life will give them satisfaction? Has anyone ever attained it that way? But even if it takes many lifetimes of seeking and enjoying sensual life, eventually the soul will turn away from it and begin the great journey towards awakening from the long dream of life and death. It is inevitable.

> "Renunciation is real power. Grasp what is meant by renunciation, for only in that there is complete rest."
>
> —Amma

It is very unusual to find a person that has truly awakened to this fact and spends all their time trying to experience the Truth of the Self. Amma would say that such a person did a lot of meritorious actions or *punyam* in their previous lives, and so, in this life, they feel a tremendous pull towards God. Nothing else makes sense or has any meaning or attraction for such a one. They are waking up from the deep, deep sleep of the Lord's Maya; they are burning with the desire to escape from the Sea of Samsara.

The greatness of Realized sages has been extolled in many holy books. They remind us of the extremely rare opportunity that we have been given to associate with Amma. By reading their words again and again, we are reminded of the Reality behind Amma's form.

In the company of sages, attachment vanishes; and with attachment, illusion. Freed from illusion, one attains steadiness, and thence liberation while yet alive. Seek therefore the company of sages.

—Sankaracharya, Bhajagovindam

Not by listening to preachers, nor by study of books, not by meritorious deeds nor by any other means can one attain that Supreme State, which is attainable only through association with the sages and the clear quest of the Self.

—Yoga Vasishta

When one has learned to love the company of sages, wherefore all these rules of discipline? When a pleasant, cool southern breeze is blowing, what need is there for a fan?

—Yoga Vasishta

Holy rivers, which are only water and idols, which are made of stone and clay, are not as mighty as the sages. For while they make one pure in the course of countless days, the sage's eyes by a mere glance purify at once.

—Srimad Bhagavatam

Amma has come to this world at this time because there is a pressing need for such a divine self-sacrificing and unconditionally loving person.

In the words of the well-known actor, Charlie Chaplin, who was, by the way, also a great humanitarian,

"We have developed speed, but we have shut ourselves in. Machinery that gives abundance has left us in want. The airplane and the radio have brought us closer together. The very nature of these inventions cries out to the goodness in men, cries out for universal brotherhood, for the unity of us all. But our knowledge has made us cynical, our cleverness hard and unkind; we think too much and feel too little. More than machinery, we need humanity; more than cleverness, we need kindness and gentleness. Without these qualities, life will be violent and all will be lost."

# CHAPTER EIGHTEEN

## *Surrender and Detachment*

Many of us have read the story of the woman who came to Lord Buddha and wanted him to bring her dead child back to life. He told her that if she could bring a mustard seed from any house that had never suffered the death of a family member, then he would perform the miracle.

She went all over the village but could not get even one mustard seed. She then realized an important truth about the nature of life—that all is transitory and ends in separation and death. Only the soul exists after death. But, even though we hear such truths, under the influence of Maya we ignore them again and again, almost immediately after hearing them.

There is an incident in the Mahabharata where the great king Yudhisthira was asked a number of questions by a yaksha, a nature spirit, as a test of the king's wisdom.

The yaksha asked: "What is the greatest wonder?"

The wise king replied: "Day after day countless people die, yet the living wish to live forever. O Lord, what can be a greater wonder?"

What a strange power this Maya is. It keeps us in a continuously forgetful state, birth after birth. Under its influence, we sink deeper and deeper into the ocean of universal delusion and are unable to understand spiritual truths however small. Even worse, we don't feel the slightest urge to wake up from this long night of deep sleep into the daylight of Divine Consciousness.

Amma shows us the way to extricate ourselves from the web of attachments to this condition. Once she told me that most people are unable to realize the simple truth that everyone loves themselves the most; we are all ultimately selfish. In the name of love, we are fooled into believing that we are dear to others and they are dear to us. It is only when we experience others' selfishness that we receive a jolt from this delusion. Amma is not discouraging us to love but rather to love without attachment, expectation and dependence, just as she is doing.

Amma: "Our attachments in the name of love always pull us down."

Devotee: What does Amma mean by that? Do you mean that my love for my wife and children is not true love? Attachment is an aspect of love, isn't it?

Amma: "Son, only a person who is completely detached can love others without any expectations. Attachment is not an aspect of real love. In real love, not only the bodies but also the souls will be united through sympathy. There will always be the knowledge of the changing or perishable nature of the body and the eternal nature of the Self. Attachment binds and destroys the person who is attached and the person to whom they are attached. Due to this attachment, discrimination fails and discipline will be absent.

"In the Mahabharata, Dhritarasthra, the blind king, was overly attached to his eldest son Duryodhana. Therefore, he could neither discipline his son nor make him think or act properly. This led to the total destruction of the king, his sons and the kingdom. As an opposite example, Sri Krishna was completely detached and could therefore love the Pandavas and, at the same time, discipline them. The story of Dhritarasthra and his son Duryodhana shows how the selfishness and attachment of one person can bring about the destruction of an entire society."

Amma tells a story about the limits of love between a husband and wife.

A woman accompanied her husband to the doctor's office. After his checkup, the doctor called the wife into his office alone.

He said, "Your husband is suffering from a very severe disease, combined with horrible stress. If you don't do the following, your husband will surely die soon. Each morning, fix him a healthy breakfast. Be pleasant and make sure he is in a good mood. For lunch make him a nutritious meal. For his dinner, prepare an especially tasty meal. Don't burden him with any chores, as he probably had a hard day. Don't discuss your problems with him, as it will only make his stress worse. And most importantly, you should satisfy his every desire and whim and let him unburden his problems on you—he should have no stress at all. Be especially loving and affectionate. If you can do this for the next ten months, I think your husband will regain his health completely."

On the way home, the husband asked his wife. "What did the doctor say?"

"You're going to die soon!"

It is a truism that almost all who come to Amma do so out of their selfish desires. Yet, even knowing this, she shows equal love to all of them, without the least expectation from anyone. This is the sign of one who lives in Divine Consciousness, the vision that all is One.

> "He is esteemed, who is of the same mind to the good-hearted, friends, foes, the indifferent, the neutral, the hateful, relatives, the righteous, and the unrighteous."
>
> —Bhagavad Gita, Ch.6, v.9

When a fruit is pulled off the tree before it is ripe, it weeps—white milk flows from its stem. But when it naturally falls off due to ripeness, there is no weeping—it just gets detached of its own accord. Because of the very nature of our minds and our life in this transitory world, we develop many attachments and consequently have to weep at the time of separation—either ours or others. This leaves wounds in our subconscious.

In the case of a deep wound, antiseptic has to be applied inside the wound after a thorough cleaning. Merely cleaning the outside and bandaging it won't do. It may get infected again and again. Similarly, practicing detachment because of our anger and pain towards one who hurts us will not work. When the anger cools down, we may get attached again, albeit keeping the wound inside.

In any case, we will probably become attached again to someone or something else soon enough. We cannot be happy without being attached to something. That something might be a person, a pet, our possessions or position. The changing and selfish nature of things is what gives us sorrow. Instead of that, we must get attached to one who won't change, who won't hurt us, who wants nothing from us, who wants only the best for us. Only God fits that description. In this perishable world where everyone is seeking his or her own happiness through love, where everyone is selfish, the fulfillment of the desire for true love will become possible only through mystic union with God, the Self of all.

This is easier said than done. God is invisible. We don't even know if such a Being actually exists, and if that Being is there, are we being heard? Isn't this a matter of faith? And how to get faith in an invisible, incomprehensible Being?

Different people conceive of God in different ways. Amma says that, whatever our conception be,

> "The Universal Power exists within you. This Supreme Truth can be attained only through faith and meditation. Just as you trust the words of scientists who talk about facts unknown to us, have faith in the words of the great Masters who speak about the Truth; they are established in that. The scriptures and the great Masters remind us that the Self, or God, is our true nature. God is not far away from us, but we need faith to imbibe this truth. God is not a limited individual who sits alone up in the clouds on a golden throne. God is Pure Consciousness that dwells within everything. Understanding this truth, learn to accept and love everyone equally."

Through divinizing the flow of thought, raising it from the lower plane of worldliness and getting established in thoughts of God and Guru, our worldly problems and suffering take on an air of triviality. Our mind becomes broad like the sky, and we gradually begin to actually feel the Divine Presence within our mind. What started as faith becomes experience. The old wounds belonging to the ego fade away. We learn to accept unavoidable painful circumstances as our Guru's blessing or gift. In her infinite wisdom, she knows what is best. All our mundane attachments dissolve in the all-embracing attachment to God.

Devotee: Some devotees say that in spite of their devotion, they still suffer.

Amma: "We call on God to fulfill our many desires. The mind is filled with desires, not with God's Form. That means that we see God as our laborer. It should not be like that. Even if God is the servant of His devotees, it is not correct for us to think of Him as such. Dedicate everything at His Feet. We must have the attitude of surrender, and then He will definitely protect us. Even after getting into the boat or bus, we won't carry the luggage, will we? We will put it down. Likewise, surrender everything to God. He will protect us. Cultivate the thought that God is near us. If there is a place to rest nearby, the mere thought of unloading the luggage which we are carrying on our head lessens the weight of the burden. If we think that there is no place to rest, then the baggage seems heavier. In the same way, when we think that God is near, all our burdens diminish."

Remembering that God is the Reality behind the world-appearance can be difficult. He is not only the unchanging One, but also the ever-active Power that makes everything happen. Creation is His play or *leela*. Sometimes we forget this and get puffed up with a sense of doership.

At the end of the Mahabharata War, Lord Krishna and Arjuna were still on the chariot. Traditionally, the charioteer was expected to come down from the chariot and, as an act of respect, hold the hand of the warrior as he stepped down. Even though Lord Krishna was God Himself, he accepted the role of charioteer and so he should have been the first one to come down from the chariot. Arjuna waited for Lord Krishna to step down, but, seeing him remain where he was, he finally stepped off by himself. He was a bit insulted at the Lord's action.

As an answer to Arjuna's ignorance, Lord Krishna stepped off the chariot and, immediately, Lord Hanuman, who was sitting in the flag, flew off and the chariot blew up in flames! Arjuna was in shock. Sri Bhagavan went on to explain that Lord Hanuman was protecting the chariot during the war from all the powerful weapons thrown at it from the opposition. He would not leave until Lord Krishna stepped off. Had Lord Krishna stepped off the chariot before Arjuna got down, Hanuman would have flown away and Arjuna would have gone up in flames with the chariot. Lord Krishna's presence was the reason why the chariot was still being held together. Arjuna's pride at having won the war and feeling that he must be honored as a great warrior blinded him to the fact that none of it would have been possible without the divine presence of Lord Krishna.

As the Lord says in the Bhagavad Gita:

> "I am the mighty world-destroying Time, now engaged in destroying the worlds. Even without thee, none of the warriors arrayed in hostile armies shalt live."

—Ch.11, v.32

### Who is God?

Perhaps it is not possible to know or understand God, but, according to the ancient books and Amma's teachings, we definitely can become one with Him by His Grace.

Once, Alexander the Great asked Diogenes, "You are so learned, you know so much. Can't you tell me something about God, what God is?"

Diogenes waited for a moment and then said, "Give me one day's time."

Alexander came the next day but again Diogenes said, "Give me two days' time," and it happened again, and he said, "give me three days' time," and then four days and then five days, and then six days and the whole week was gone.

Alexander was annoyed and said, "What do you mean

by this? If you don't know the answer, you should have told me before. If you know, then what is the explanation for the delay?"

Diogenes said, "That moment you asked me, I thought that I knew. But the more I tried to catch hold of it, the more it became elusive. The more I thought about it, the farther away it was. Right now, I don't know anything, and the only thing I can say to you is, that those who think they know God, they know not."

I once heard a devotee arguing with a mahatma, saying that, in the Non-dual experience of samadhi, God disappears. The mahatma said, "It is not like that. He doesn't disappear, but *you* will and He alone will remain!"

Sometimes we will be given chances to test our faith. On one of Amma's tours in the US, the tour group was to meet at the airport and fly to the next city. Somehow, Swami Purnamritananda and I, along with two other devotees, were dropped off at the wrong airport. We did not realize what had happened until we reached the gate and no plane was there. We didn't have any money or even the tickets. The flight was due to leave in ten minutes. We tried to get a taxi to take us to the other airport, but no driver would agree to take us such a short distance. We all thought, 'Okay, Amma. If you want us to travel with you, you will have to act fast.' We stood there by the curb waiting, hoping against hope.

Just then, a car pulled up at the curb. It was the same devotee who had dropped us off and was now coming from the other airport. She rushed us there; we ran to the plane and, just as we got inside, the door shut! We all let out a sigh—Ammaaaaaaa!

## Responsibility

> Amma will clear the path to Liberation. She will hold your hand and lead you to the goal. Be truthful and carry out your life's responsibilities, and in this way you will attain peace of mind.
>
> —Amma

When someone makes a promise, we usually have our suspicions aroused. Politicians make promises in order to get into power. The lover promises the beloved something in order to secure his or her own pleasure. The parents make promises to get the children to do things that they will not easily agree to, and the children make promises to the parents to get out of doing what they are supposed to do.

These people all have their own agendas in mind, their own selfish reasons for making promises, and they may not even have the power to fulfill them. Amma's promise is not like that. She says that she will clear our path to Liberation and, holding our hand, lead us to the goal. It is hard to imagine what is the power or inner experience that gives her the confidence to make such a promise. If we go deeper into Amma's words, we will find that our understanding of her may not be all that we think it is.

Amma says she will clear our path and hold our hand and lead us to the goal of Liberation from the cycle of birth and death. How is she going to do these things? Surely that is possible only if she is living in that state herself.

For the majority of us, Amma is the person who is sitting in Amritapuri in India and who also travels around the world every year. So how can she possibly fulfill her promise? It is certainly not physically possible. Can she do it through something like remote control? Even if that is the case, how can she attend to all the millions of her devotees at the same time? What if some devotees simultaneously need her? How can she hear everyone at the same time and know what each one requires at any particular time? It is all so mind-boggling!!

Some remotes can control many appliances at once, all from a small unit. Of course, unless we happen to be a rocket scientist or computer programmer, we find even that task complicated and difficult to do. Many of us are not very technical or mechanical minded. Once, someone doing computer work at the ashram called me urgently. They said that the printer did not work any-more. They did everything right and still it was as dead as a doornail. When I arrived, I noticed that the printer wasn't even turned on!

If we want to understand Amma's words, we must give up the idea that she is a mere body of flesh and bones, endowed with a limited mind just like ours. If she can take care of all of us, she must be here and now with each one of us, though invisible to our physical eyes. Her experience of her Self must be very different than ours. In her own mysterious way, she can clear all obstacles and help us along.

The Bhagavad Gita says:

> "By Me all this world is pervaded, My form unmanifested. All beings dwell in Me, and I do not dwell in them.

> "Nor do those beings dwell in Me; behold My Divine Yoga! Sustaining all the beings, but not dwelling in them, is My Self, the Cause of beings.

> "As the mighty wind moving everywhere rests ever in space, so, know thou, do all beings rest in Me."

> —Ch.9,v.4-6.

And again,

> "By devotion he knows Me in truth, what and who I am; then, knowing Me in truth, he forthwith enters into Me.

"Doing continually all actions whatsoever, taking refuge in Me,—by My Grace he reaches the eternal undecaying Abode.

"Mentally resigning all deeds to Me, regarding Me as the Supreme, resorting to mental concentration, do thou ever fix thy heart in Me.

"Fixing thy heart in Me, thou shalt, by My Grace, cross over all difficulties; but if from egotism thou will not hear (Me), thou shalt perish.

"Hear thou again My word supreme, the most secret of all; because thou art My firm friend, therefore will I tell thee what is good.

"Fix thy thought on Me, be devoted to Me, worship Me, do homage to Me. Thou shalt reach Myself. This truth do I declare to thee; (for) thou art dear to Me."

—Ch.18, v.55-58,64-65

And finally,

"And whoso, at the time of death, thinking of Me alone, leaves the body and goes forth, he reaches My being; there is no doubt in this.

"Of whatever Being thinking at the end a man leaves the body, Him alone, O son of Kunti, reaches he by whom the thought of that Being has been constantly dwelt upon.

"Therefore at all times do thou meditate on Me and fight: with mind and reason fixed on Me thou shalt doubtless come to Me alone."

—Ch.8, v.5-7

Obviously, this does not mean we will have no suffering after seeking refuge in Amma; but just as a parent holds the hand of a child as it struggles to walk and doesn't let it fall down and get hurt, similarly she will hold us with her all-pervading hands if we follow her instructions. For this reason, we must study her teachings to know what her instructions are both in a general way and anything that is specifically for us. That is the fine print at the end of the contract!

# CHAPTER NINETEEN

## Truthfulness and Responsibility

Why is truth given so much value by the sages? Relative truth is a reflection in Nature of the absolute transcendent Truth or Brahman. We tell lies in order to protect our ego, in order to gain something. The ego is the very antithesis of the Supreme Truth. It veils the Truth from our vision and makes us feel as if we are separate beings. It is a big lie. By abiding by the truth, we attenuate some part of the ego and progress spiritually.

There can be no exceptions to this rule when interacting with Amma. Even a white lie should not be told to her. Lying is quite natural for humans. We do it all the time, trying to make ourselves look good, never at fault. These are all the workings of the ego. We may not hesitate to lie even to the Truth Itself in the form of Amma. We cannot fool her. We cannot even exaggerate to her. She always knows the truth of a person or situation. Instead of making us look good, we end up making ourselves look very bad by exaggerating or lying to her. It betrays our lack of trust in her. It kills our innocence and devotion.

It shows that we have more devotion towards our ego than towards God, and our innocence is replaced with crookedness. We must be extremely alert not to act with Amma the way we act "out there."

Some lawyers may be having some doubt as to how they can continue after hearing this. One lawyer asked Amma,

> Lawyer: "What is our fate, Amma? We are walking around getting involved in court cases, quarrels, lies, etc."

> Amma: "That is all right, son; it is the dharma (duty) of a lawyer to argue for his party in a suit. That is not wrong. A lawyer is only performing his duty when he argues for a criminal. Even then, accept only truthful cases as far as possible. The sin does not go to the lawyer if the criminal is saved by the arguments put forth by him. The criminal is only saved from the court of law; he cannot escape from God's court. One must bear the fruit of one's actions.

> "Just like anyone else, a lawyer can also come to spirituality, abandoning worldly life after the dawn of real vairagya (detachment) has risen in him. Until then, svadharma (one's own dharma) should be performed dedicating everything to God.

"In the olden days there was only truth. All families led a truthful life. Even though someone might be a servant, he would not give up truth even if somebody offered millions to him. If you hold on to truth, everything else will come to you. Without truth, nothing good can exist. Truth is everything. Truth is God."

The other quality that Amma asks us to develop is a sense of responsibility. She says this from her own experience. She has always acted in a responsible way. Even though she lives in a sublime plane beyond body-consciousness and has no attachment to anyone, she still does what she feels is her duty.

In the days before the ashram existed, she looked after her family and other relatives, even if it meant great hardship to herself. When her father was sick in the hospital, even though she was already giving darshan in Krishna Bhava in those days, she would do all the household chores, in addition to cooking for him and taking the food all the way to the hospital thirty-five kilometers away. In order to get to the bus in town, she would have to pass by a number of abusive people, who would shout at her and even throw stones at her, calling out "Hey Krishna, Hey Krishna" in ridicule. That never stopped her from doing her duty. Amma's life has been a constant and compassionate discharge of her duty towards humanity, regardless of the suffering she has to bear. She has always been conscious of her duty, mundane or spiritual. We can see the teachings of karma yoga fully manifest in her: Do your duty and surrender the fruits to God. And be prepared to die doing so.

Amma feels that her life is for comforting suffering *jivas* (individuals) and putting them on the path towards liberation from the cycle of birth and death. She takes this duty so seriously that she continues to put her body through unimaginable strain and suffering even more today than ever before. As we all know, it is not unusual for her to sit eighteen hours or more at a stretch comforting those who come to her for solace.

Amma tells us to do sadhana regularly, but she also asks us to divinize our daily life. If we don't do that, peace of mind may be out of our reach. The peace that we get during sadhana has to be brought into our daily life. After all, it is our daily life that distracts us so much. We must find ways to think of God during all hours.

### Lady Advised to See God in her Grandchild

An old lady came with her grandson to a mahatma and asked him if it would be all right for her to renounce her family and move to Brindavan, the childhood residence of Lord Krishna, for doing sadhana? Was it advisable for her to break all family ties?

The sage replied, "Please listen carefully. What is it that looks at you through the eyes of your grandson? What force or energy is it that pours through every pore of his body?"

"It must be God, of course," said the lady.

"When you go to Brindavan, you will have to worship one Deity day and night, the image of Sri Krishna. Isn't this child's body just as good an image of Krishna as the stone image in Brindavan?" asked the swami.

The woman was taken aback for a moment and then thought that the saint must be right. Why go to Brindavan when she could just as well worship God through the body of her grandchild? Was it not God who looked through his eyes, spoke through his mouth and made all the functions of his body take place?

Sounded easy enough, but then came the catch. The saint told her, "You must no longer look upon the child as your grandson. You are no longer related to him in any way. You must look upon him as the Lord and break all sense of family and worldly ties with him. The only tie should be between you and God in this boy. Give all the love in your heart to God in this form. This is real renunciation."

Amma doesn't ask us to give up the world. She asks us to give up our worldly attachments and ties. The friend, the wife and the husband should cease to be as such. We should see only God in all. Even our negative feeling towards our enemies and wicked people must be renounced and Divinity seen in them. Our worldly vision must be transformed into the Vision of God in all. All personal relationships must be sublimated to the level of a universal relationship with God. Amma is the very embodiment of this truth and the greatest example for us to follow.

Amma says,

> "Having attained human form, we should elevate ourselves to the Divine. We should surrender our individual selves to God and thus become perfect. Nothing is impossible for Maya, children. Don't fall into the calamity called Maya. Don't become victims of illusion and lament. Free your mind from its clutches."

It is after many, many lifetimes as sub-human species that we are at last endowed with a human form and given a chance by the Creator to attain union with the Him. In fact, the final goal, the true aim of evolution, is to unite with the Creator of evolution. Amma and the scriptures tell us that we can never ever be truly happy unless our oneness with the Creator is experienced. Creation, however vast and wonderful, can never fill the bottomless pit of our longing for unending, ever-new, exquisite happiness.

*Oru nimishm engilum* (Even for a Moment) is a popular song that Amma sings. It means,

> O man, do you feel peace of mind for even a second while seeking happiness in this world?

> Without grasping the Truth, you run after the shadow of Maya. You will face the same fate as that of a moth deluded by the sight of a glowing fire.

> Having evolved gradually through various incarnations like worms, crawling creatures of different kinds, birds and animals, you become a human being. What is the purpose of human life other than Self-Realization?

> Cast away lust, pride and greed. Leave the life of illusion and spend your human birth singing the glory of the Supreme Brahman. God-Realization is your birthright; don't waste away this precious life.

# CHAPTER TWENTY

## Man—the Glory of Creation

### Intuition Versus Instinct

The scriptures of India tell us that, among all living things, man alone is endowed with discrimination making him superior to all others. Hearing this truth, the animals in a forest had their own doubts as to its veracity. The cunning fox was vexed at the glorification of man and his exalted position in God's creation. It thought within itself, 'Am I in any way less intelligent than man? Or is he less cunning than I am when he wants to cheat others? He is a living creature just as much as I am. In fact, I am more contented than he. I don't wear costly or a variety of clothes every season. I endure heat and cold patiently. I do not ask for umbrellas to protect me from the rain, or dark glasses to prevent the glare of the sunlight in summer. I do not ask for a motor car or train to go from place to place. Though we animals possess all these and many more noble qualities, why should man be considered as superior to us? I shall see that this injustice is put to an end.'

The fox ran hither and thither inciting other animals to join him. He was able to gather a number of them. Then they all went to the elephant. The wise elephant said, "Brothers, there is no doubt some truth in what you say. Let us then go to another forest dweller and ascertain his views. There lives a sage in yonder cottage. Let us go to him and represent our case."

They all agreed to the elephant's suggestion. "Swami, you know me well," barked the dog. "I am the symbol of gratitude. If a man beats me a thousand times and gives me a morsel of food but once, I am grateful to him throughout my life, and ready to give up my life in his service. But man forgets a thousand services rendered to him and remembers the one wrong that his friend might have done. Completely ignoring the help received, he is ready to murder his kith and kin if he is wronged once, even unwittingly. How then can you say that man is superior to beasts?"

And this was the cow's plea: "Man takes me to the pastures to graze. Sometimes he gives me a little straw or husk. In return I give him my nourishing milk. Sometimes he even starves my baby in order to feed himself and his children. When I thus feed him and his family, he gives me shelter in a foul-smelling and unclean place in the backyard of his house. The moment I go dry, I am ill-treated and ignored. If I become old, I am driven out or sold to a butcher. Such is man whom you exalt sky-high. Please, tell me why."

Now it was the crow's turn: "Has man got this one quality that I possess? Even if a small crumb of bread is thrown to me, I caw and call all my brothers and sisters to share it with them. But man does just the opposite. However much he has, he hoards still more and even goes out of his way to snatch the bread of his neighbor. How can this selfish and greedy man be exalted above me?"

The fish whispered: "O sage! I shall not call man inferior to me, but I call him downright foolish! I cause him no harm. In fact, I serve him by keeping the ponds, tanks, lakes and rivers clean. I eat away the dirt that is thrown into the water by him. But instead of preserving such a good benefactor, this foolish man catches me and kills and eats me! Do you regard this foolish man superior to me?"

The mule brayed: "The fish is quite right. Look at my pitiable plight. I am a beast of burden. I am famous for the divine quality of patience. I bear insult and injury patiently. Without my service, the people in the hills will perish for want of the necessities of life. I carry their food and other goods. What is my reward? Beating and more beating! Is this man superior to me?"

"Tell him everything, friends, tell him all about your qualities and your superhuman attainments," chimed in the cunning fox.

"Sir," said the deer, "the very skin on which you sit and meditate on God belongs to our kind. Have you ever heard of man's skin being put to any good use? In the matter of beauty, the most beautiful eyes of a damsel are often compared to mine. My lovely horns decorate man's halls."

"So also," said the peacock, "my feathers are so charming that even Lord Krishna had them tucked into His turban. Lord Shanmukha uses me as His Vehicle, and many of His devotees use my feathers as magic wands to drive off evil spirits. No one has ever heard of man's skin or hair being so used."

"All my excretions are considered holy and highly purificatory," said the cow. "The *panchagavya* is an invariable item in all the holy rites of man. The very mention of human excretions will induce only vomiting in man and the least contact with them has to be followed by a thorough wash and bath."

"Can any man boast of having such a wonderful sense of smell as I have?" enquired the dog.

"Can any man boast of having such a wonderful sense of sight as I have?" asked the hawk.

"Can any man see during the night and the day with equal ease as I can?" asked the cat.

"I can do great things. I have an enormous body. There are numberless stories of my intelligence. My tusks and bones are converted into lovely ivory images and idols. All this is true, but kindly enlighten us as to why man is considered superior to us. Though I do agree with the arguments of my brothers, I feel that there must be some wise reason for this," said the elephant.

All the animals waited patiently to listen to the sage. The sage said, "Listen, my kinsmen of the jungle! All that you have said is true. But God has endowed man with the eye of discrimination, the intellect, which distinguishes the right from the wrong, the truth from the untruth, the good from the evil. You are governed by instinct. Man can attain intuition. He can control his instincts and, through intuition, attain God."

"And if he doesn't?" asked the cunning fox.

"If he doesn't, he is of course worse than a beast. If he does, he is far superior to all else in creation," said the sage.

Hearing this, the animals went away satisfied.

### The American Dream

Many people the world over think that living "the American dream" will make them happy. What exactly is the American dream? There are many definitions, but they all seem to boil down to this:

> A set of ideals in which freedom includes the opportunity for prosperity and success, and an upward social mobility for the family and children, achieved through hard work in a society with few barriers.

Even in America, many school-going children are now seeing through the hollowness of the American dream of getting a nice house, job, car and other material pleasures. They feel that good relationships are more important than any material object.

The problem with that analysis is that it doesn't go far enough, because relationships can also sour and become painful or hollow.

Of course, Amma also feels that material wealth and pleasures are important goals in life. Look at all of her charitable projects. They try to provide people with at least the minimum of necessities and opportunities to lead a happy life. But she also says that only the relationship with God will satisfy the longing of the human heart for happiness. The closer one comes to God, the more one enjoys divine bliss and peace. That is the experience of all devotees down the ages.

Mahatmas, past and present, say that when the soul is nearing the completion of its round of births and deaths, it develops a distaste for the world. That eventually leads one to devotion to God. It seems to be a law of nature that, at that time, one gets a Guru to show one the way to awakening from the Universal Illusion.

What is it that keeps us travelling in the cycle of births and deaths? Maya hides the Creator and projects the creation, and that blinds us to our true nature as the imperishable soul and makes us feel that we are the perishable body.

Amma says again and again that we shouldn't be satisfied with the status quo. We must associate with awakened souls so that we become dissatisfied with Maya and strive to wake up. The saying that "Birds of a feather flock together" is so true.

The great sage, Adi Shankaracharya, whose teachings on Advaita Vedanta (or Non-duality) are accepted as their own by Amma and other contemporary mahatmas like Sri Ramana Maharshi, wrote many devotional and Advaitic hymns. In one of these, Bhaja Govindam, he tells us about the greatness of association with sages.

*Satsangatve nissangatvam*
*Nissangatve nirmohatvam*
*Nirmohatve nishchalatattvam*
*Nishchalatattve jeevanmukti*

The company of the good weans one away from false attachments; from non-attachment comes freedom from delusion, when delusion ends, the mind becomes unwavering and steady and from an unwavering and steady mind comes Jivanmukti (liberation in this life).

He tells us that crossing samsara, the ocean of life and death, is impossible except with the help of God.

*Punarapi jananam punarapi maranam*
*Punarapi janani jathare shayanam*
*Iha samsare bahudustare*
*Kripayapare pahi murare*

Again and again one is born,
And again and again one dies,
And again and again one sleeps in the mother's womb.
Help me to cross this impassable, limitless sea of Life, my Lord.

Maya makes us like sheep. For the most part, we do whatever everyone else is doing. A rare person thinks about the ultimate end of their actions. Death and the company of sages shake us awake and makes us think deeply about our life.

### Swami Vivekananda and a Student

Swami Vivekananda was sailing to America for the second time. On the ship, he met an Indian student who was also going to America for higher studies. The student looked very sophisticated and behaved arrogantly, as very few people went abroad those days. The swami thought that this would be the right time to give him proper values in life. So, one evening, when they met on deck, Swamiji asked the student,

"Son, what are you going to America for?"

"I am going for higher studies, sir. It will take four to five years."

"Then what will happen?"

"I will return to India. I am sure to get a very good job and earn a lot of money."

"Then?"

The student was surprised. Was the swami so ignorant that he did not know the value of money?

"Then sir, I shall be the most fortunate person. All the fathers of marriageable girls will come to me with proposals. I will be in a position to dictate my own terms and marry the girl of my choice."

"Then?"

The student felt irritated by these questions, but he did not show it. However, he answered impatiently,

"Then, Sir, when we live together, there will be children. I shall become a big officer; we will have a bungalow to live in and a car to drive. The children will get the best education and all opportunities to do well in life. My daughters will make good matches and my sons may even go abroad for higher studies and land good jobs."

"Then?"

Now the student was certain the swami was mocking him. He looked at his face to see his expression, but it was dead-pan. So, with mounting irritation, the student said,

"Sir, by the time my children are settled in life, I shall be nearing the age of retirement. So I will build a small house in my village and live there after retirement and get a good pension and manage quite comfortably."

"Then?"

The student lost control this time. He retorted angrily,

"What sort of questions are you asking? What more is there to say? Then I will die!"

The swami smiled calmly and said,

"If it is only to earn, eat, produce children and then one day die, what is human life worth? Are not the animals doing the same without foreign education? Are not the birds doing the same without schooling? Are not the fish doing the same thing without high salaries and bungalows? Birth and death are common to all beings. No doubt, one should live a decent life, but one should always have high ideals. It is fine to have money and position, but only worthwhile if it is used in the service of others."

The student felt ashamed, and from that day onwards, resolved to lead a purposeful life in the service of society.

Of course, if the swami was able to spend more time with this man, he no doubt would have gradually directed his mind to more spiritual thoughts and higher goals like Amma is doing.

If we have misplaced a thing, what do we do to find it? We keep it in mind until it dawns on us where it is. Similarly, Amma says that we have now "misplaced" God amongst all our occupations and possessions; in other words, this world. To find Him, we must keep Him in mind. We must also remember that He is within us, hidden by our endless thoughts and feelings. Finding Him within us is the greatest joy, the end of all suffering, the dawn of supreme bliss.

There are many ways to keep Him in mind, like meditation, japa, bhajans, seva and so on. But to a few rare devotees, the great good fortune comes in the form of being a contemporary of a Divine Soul. The *Yoga Sutras of Patanjali* says that thinking of a mahatma is a very natural and effective form of meditation, which will purify the restless mind. Great souls like Krishna, Rama, Buddha, Jesus and Sri Ramakrishna attracted countless souls through their divine magnetism. Many souls attained mental purity and found God through their association with those mahatmas. We are similarly blessed with Amma's divine presence, and our chances of reaching God are also as good as those blessed souls. But we must empty our mind of its preoccupation with the world and fill it with the thought of God or Guru. At some point, the revelation that the Guru is within, and is our own most beloved Self, will dawn.

The residents of Brindavan, the gopis and the gopas, had this natural kind of devotion for Lord Sri Krishna. Even though they were leading their day to day lives, the thought of Krishna was always in the back of their minds. In order to strengthen their faith and devotion, the Lord performed many big and small miracles.

Advanced sadhaks don't need any miracles or reassurances of their Guru's divine nature. They can always feel the intense peace and bliss that radiates from the Guru's person. But the rest of us ordinary humans need an occasional reassurance. If we are alert, we gradually realize that we are frequently experiencing miracles of Amma's grace. To see things in that light, we must accept both the pleasant and the painful as her grace.

Look closely at your life. Amma is always with you, teaching you, drawing your mind towards her. Don't be afraid. Be brave and have faith in Amma's words, that "I am always with you, my child." She will be with us, now and for all eternity.

# Book Catalog
## *By Author*

**Sri Mata Amritanandamayi Devi**

108 Quotes On Faith
108 Quotes On Love
Compassion, The Only Way To Peace:
    Paris Speech
Cultivating Strength And Vitality
Living In Harmony
May Peace And Happiness Prevail:
    Barcelona Speech
May Your Hearts Blossom:
    Chicago Speech
Practice Spiritual Values And Save The
    World: Delhi Speech
The Awakening Of Universal Motherhood:
    Geneva Speech
The Eternal Truth
The Infinite Potential Of Women:
    Jaipur Speech
Understanding And Collaboration
    Between Religions
Unity Is Peace: Interfaith Speech

**Swami Amritaswarupananda Puri**

Ammachi: A Biography
Awaken Children, Volumes 1-9
From Amma's Heart
Mother Of Sweet Bliss
The Color Of Rainbow

**Swami Jnanamritananda Puri**

Eternal Wisdom, Volumes 1-2

**Swami Paramatmananda Puri**

Dust Of Her Feet
On The Road To Freedom Volumes 1-2
Talks, Volumes 1-6

**Swami Purnamritananda Puri**

Unforgettable Memories

**Swami Ramakrishnananda Puri**

Eye Of Wisdom
Racing Along The Razor's Edge
Secret Of Inner Peace
The Blessed Life
The Timeless Path
Ultimate Success

**Swamini Krishnamrita Prana**

Love Is The Answer
Sacred Journey
The Fragrance Of Pure Love
Torrential Love

**M.A. Center Publications**

1,000 Names Commentary
Archana Book (Large)
Archana Book (Small)
Being With Amma
Bhagavad Gita
Bhajanamritam, Volumes 1-6
Embracing The World
For My Children
Immortal Light
Lead Us To Purity
Lead Us To The Light
Man And Nature
My First Darshan
Puja: The Process Of Ritualistic
    Worship
Sri Lalitha Trishati Stotram

# Amma's Websites

**AMRITAPURI—Amma's Home Page**
*Teachings, Activities, Ashram Life, eServices, Yatra, Blogs and News*
http://www.amritapuri.org

**AMMA (Mata Amritanandamayi)**
*About Amma, Meeting Amma, Global Charities, Groups and Activities and Teachings*
http://www.amma.org

**EMBRACING THE WORLD®**
*Basic Needs, Emergencies, Environment, Research and News*
http://www.embracingtheworld.org

**AMRITA UNIVERSITY**
*About, Admissions, Campuses, Academics, Research, Global and News*
http://www.amrita.edu

**THE AMMA SHOP—Embracing the World® Books & Gifts Shop**
*Blog, Books, Complete Body, Home & Gifts, Jewelry, Music and Worship*
http://www.theammashop.org

**IAM—Integrated Amrita Meditation Technique®**
*Meditation Taught Free of Charge to the Public, Students, Prisoners and Military*
http://www.amma.org/groups/north-america/projects/iam-meditation-classes

**AMRITA PUJA**
*Types and Benefits of Pujas, Brahmasthanam Temple, Astrology Readings, Ordering Pujas*
http://www.amritapuja.org

**GREENFRIENDS**
*Growing Plants, Building Sustainable Environments, Education and Community Building*
http://www.amma.org/groups/north-america/projects/green-friends

**FACEBOOK**
*This is the Official Facebook Page to Connect with Amma*
https://www.facebook.com/MataAmritanandamayi

**DONATION PAGE**
*Please Help Support Amma's Charities Here:*
http://www.amma.org/donations

CPSIA information can be obtained
at www.ICGtesting.com
Printed in the USA
FSOW03n1757271015
12652FS